NURSES AT WAR

Nurses at War

Women on the Frontline 1939-45

Penny Starns

ISIS
LARGE PRINT
Oxford and Orlando

First published in Great Britain 2000
by Sutton Publishing Ltd.

Published in Large Print 2001 by ISIS Publishing Ltd,
7 Centremead, Osney Mead, Oxford OX2 0ES
by arrangement with Sutton Publishing

British Library Cataloguing in Publication Data
Starns, Penny
   Nurses at war : women on the frontline, 1939-45. –
   Large print ed.
   1. World War, 1939-1945 – Great Britain – Medical care
   2. World War, 1939-1945 – Participation, Female 3. Military
   nursing – Great Britain – History 4. World War, 1939-1945 –
   Personal narratives, British 5. Large type books
   I. Title
   940.5'475'41'0922

ISBN 0-7531-5498-6 (hb)
ISBN 0-7531-5499-4 (pb)

Printed and bound by Antony Rowe, Chippenham and Reading

CONTENTS

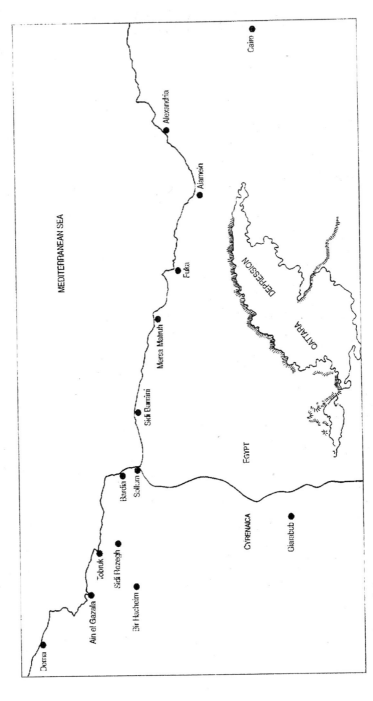

North Africa

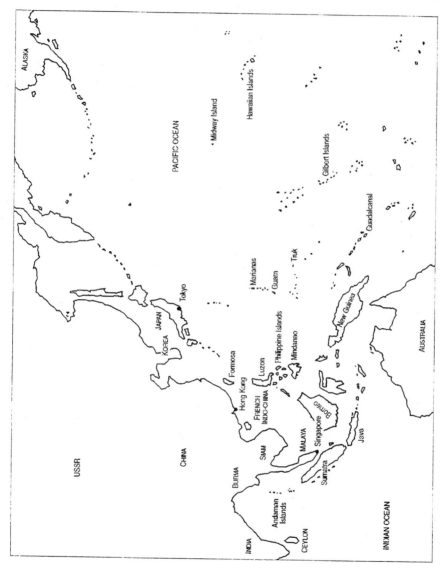

The Pacific

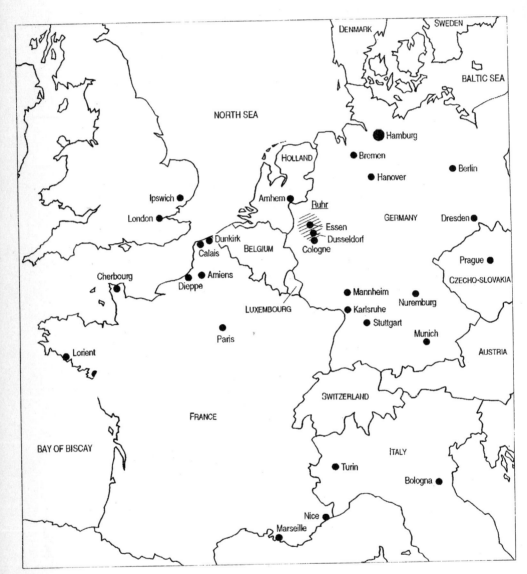

Western Europe

*Dedicated to the memory of
Dr Monica Baly*

LIST OF ABBREVIATIONS

AHM	Association of Hospital Matrons
ATS	Auxiliary Territorial Service
BRCS	British Red Cross Society
CNR	Civil Nursing Reserve
GNC	General Nursing Council
IWM	Imperial War Museum
NHS	National Health Service
PMRAFNS	Princess Mary's Royal Air Force Nursing Service
PRO	Public Record Office
QAIMNS	Queen Alexandra's Imperial Military Nursing Service
QARANC	Queen Alexandra's Royal Army Nursing Corps
QARNNS	Queen Alexandra's Royal Naval Nursing Service
RAMC	Royal Army Medical Corps
RCN	Royal College of Nursing
RE	Royal Engineers
SEAN	State Enrolled Assistant Nurse
SGD	Surgeon General Doctor
SRN	State Registered Nurse
TANS	Territorial Army Nursing Service
UNRRA	United Nations Relief and Rehabilitation Administration
VAD	Voluntary Aid Detachment

WAAF	Women's Auxiliary Air Force
WHO	World Health Organisation
WO	War Office
WRAC	Women's Royal Army Corps

ACKNOWLEDGEMENTS

The most important people to acknowledge in this book are the nurses who recounted their experiences for my research and for the BBC Radio 4 programme *Frontline Females*. They are: Monica Baly, Mary Bates, Glenys Branson, Constance Collingwood, Gertrude Cooper, Ursula Dowling, Brenda Fuller, Anne Gallimore, Monica Goulding, Daphne Ingram, Anita Kelly, Margaret Kneebone, Sylvia Mayo, Kay McCormack, Anne Moat, Phyllis Thoms and Margot Turner.

Special thanks are due to Monica Baly, to whom this book is dedicated, for her kindness, friendship and guidance in the field of nursing history. Monica remained a very dear friend and mentor until her death in 1998. I wish also to record my thanks to Cynthia Enloe, whose book *Does Khaki Become You?* has greatly influenced my work and who has offered assistance and encouragement far beyond the call of academic duty. Roger Cooter and Mark Harrison have also supported my work.

I am greatly indebted to Bob Moore, Phil Ollerenshaw and Rodney Lowe for their undergraduate and postgraduate supervision of my career, and to the University of Bristol for giving me the scholarship funding that made my research possible. Archivists Susan McGann, Jonathan Evans, Elizabeth Boardman and Major McCombe have offered invaluable assistance and Mary Tosh has been responsible for patiently transcribing the oral history tapes. I am also indebted to those who agreed to read the first drafts of this book and offer their critical comments: these include Joan Starns, Jo Denman, and Ann Starr.

During the early stages of my research Colonel Gruber von Arnis of the Queen Alexandra's Royal Army Nursing Corps ensured that I was given a valuable insight into the life of military nurses, for which I am very grateful. This gratitude is also extended to the History Society of the Royal College of Nursing.

I acknowledge my parents, Edward and Joan Starns, and Lynda and Chris Starns for their encouragement and practical support, and Roger Middleton for his unequivocal intellectual stimulation.

Finally, I thank my sons James, Michael and Lewis for providing me with love, understanding and an unparalleled sense of humour which has sustained me throughout my research.

INTRODUCTION

This book is essentially the story of a remarkable and courageous group of women who nursed both at home and abroad during the Second World War. It charts their emotional highs and lows, and follows them through nearly every theatre of war.

It is also a story which, for the most part, is told by nurses themselves. Moreover, by placing this story firmly within the context of the political developments of the time, it is hoped that the reader will understand not just the difficult working conditions faced by all nurses throughout the war, but also their wider ambitions for professional recognition.

The research for this book was originally conducted as part of a broader study that examined the links between the British military and civilian nursing professions. Hitherto, with the exception of Anne Summers's book, *Angels and Citizens*, which records nursing history in the period leading up to the First World War, there were no accounts that related the experiences of military nurses to civilian society. Because the experiences of military and civilian nurses had, up to this time, been recorded as separate entities, an accepted view of nursing history emerged. This view maintained that British nursing developed by adopting a series of professional and educational strategies in order to gain credibility and status. It is a view which this book challenges. Far from obtaining status by educational means, nurses actually turned to the military in order to raise and protect their registered status. This military identification became more intense from 1939 onwards and provided an obstacle to civilian nursing reform. The militarisation of nursing was also detrimental to patient care.

But for registered nurses who worked throughout the Second World War and faced professional erosion on a daily basis, there were not many options. In her excellent work *Reconstructing Women's Wartime Lives*, Penny Summerfield identified two main groups of women: those who embraced the war and those who endured the war. In the main, nurses fell into the group which embraced the war, believing that it offered new opportunities both to expand nursing practice and to demonstrate the value of their professional skills. Their initial enthusiasm, however, was dampened by government moves that seriously undermined their already precarious professional standing. Subsequently, the ways in which nurses chose to protect their profession were at best unorthodox and at worst misguided. Backed into a corner by the erosion of their professional credentials, nurses increasingly looked to their military counterparts for guidance.

Perhaps for a profession with strong military roots this appeal for military inspiration was not surprising. But within the context of a body of women dedicated to healing the sick and relieving their suffering, the fact that nurses expected the military to provide the answers to their status problems appeared incongruous to say the least. Nevertheless, nurses chose to adopt a process of increased military identification in an attempt to reassert their professional status, although this process needs to be viewed within the context of the overall militarisation of British society at this time. This was, after all, a time when even librarians were asking to wear military uniform!

Nonetheless, although nurses were a part of this overall trend they also adopted their own distinct militarisation policy. The leading protagonist of this policy was Dame Katherine Jones, Matron-in-Chief of the Army. Dame Katherine's main goal was to link the registered nurse with the military "officer class", and to this end she waged an all-out battle to achieve commissioned officer status for military registered nurses. More importantly, Dame Katherine believed that registered nurse status would be further secured by imposing the Army framework on civilian nursing.

Military nurses also had their own status problems, however, and the process of militarisation was not merely motivated by the need to raise civilian nurse status; it was also introduced as a means of gaining equality with the rest of the women's services. The armed forces had established women's services, which had rapidly overtaken military nurses in terms of pay and status. Thus the militarisation of nurses was considered essential if nurses were to avoid being outstripped in every sense by the women's services.

As an integral part of Dame Katherine's militarisation policy, nurses were moved up with the fighting forces to work at the frontline in operational areas. Nurses had found themselves working on the frontline of battle on previous occasions, but this was more often by accident than by design. It is perhaps also appropriate to state at this point that while members of the Royal Army Medical Corps (RAMC) also worked on the frontline, performed an equal amount of heroic deeds and suffered the consequences in much the same way as military nurses, this book is essentially about the latter.

This is primarily because the issues that surround women working on the frontline are still contested. Male military officers remain divided as to the value of women working in operational areas, and this divided opinion is not unique to the British military. As Cynthia Enloe has noted in *Does Khaki Become You?*, her exceptional account of the militarisation of women's lives, the American military has often pretended that women were nowhere near the battle lines in various conflicts despite evidence to the contrary.

Furthermore, throughout her work Enloe has successfully demonstrated on countless occasions how military forces manipulated women during both war and peace conditions, in the same way as British Army officers considered soldiers' wives to be the useful poor of the regiment. But in the case of British military nurses, the situation was somewhat different. Military nurses were actually trying to manipulate the military. They were playing the military game, attempting to assimilate fully within the military framework, protocol and belief systems in an effort to gain full recognition for their nursing services. They honestly believed that they were achieving goals that would benefit themselves, their patients and their civilian colleagues.

That nurses should have to adopt such extreme measures in order to gain professional recognition, however, suggested that women still needed to justify their existence by desperately identifying with masculinity in all its guises. The role of the military nurse was unique, if only by virtue of the fact that she was dedicated to saving life while simultaneously working within an organisation that was equally dedicated to taking life. But this did not mean that the military nurse should necessarily succumb to military doctrine or behaviour. When Florence Nightingale established military nursing she did so in an attempt to introduce a more gentle civilian nursing service into a harsh military environment. The militarisation of the nursing services during the Second World War brought about a complete reversal of this original objective.

However, before readers embark on the main body of the text it is perhaps useful for them to understand precisely why nurses were so concerned with their status; what in practice militarisation offered them in terms of elevating this status; and, furthermore, what the implications of militarisation were for nursing practice and the quality of patient care in both civilian and military nursing fields. Nursing aims from 1939 onwards were twofold: firstly, to maintain adequate standards of patient care and, secondly, to protect and raise their professional status. The two were not always compatible. In order to appreciate the nurses' dilemma and what they perceived to be the solution it is necessary to consider briefly the historical background to nursing development before 1939.

For much of the nineteenth century British nursing lacked a clear professional identity. The sick were cared for more often by relatives and friends than by people in possession of recognisable nursing skills. Additional care was provided when necessary by religious sisterhoods and domestic handywomen. Military nursing was a male domain as women were considered too delicate to withstand the rigours of war and care for severely injured men. Then, during the Crimean War, Florence Nightingale was allowed to take a party of female nurses to nurse the troops in Scutari. Despite the myths that have surrounded the Nightingale legend, the War Office was not fully convinced of the value of female nurses until after the Boer War. Nevertheless, a grateful public donated money to a Nightingale fund, which was used to establish nurse training schools at Netley (military) and at St Thomas's Hospital. Consequently, military and civilian nursing sectors became inextricably linked, and what became known as the Nightingale system provided the basis for a secular form of nurse training that had been widely accepted by the turn of the nineteenth century. The military values incorporated into the Nightingale system revolved around a sense of self-sacrifice, duty, discipline and respect for authority.

Since nurses needed to conform to Victorian ideas of class and gender, nurses' homes were established to provide a safe cultural environment for middle-class women. But although Nightingale had advocated one portal of entry for nurse training, hospitals favoured a two-tiered system. The emerging profession was, therefore, divided between middle- and upper-class ladies, who paid for their instruction, and the working-class girls, who undertook more of the menial tasks and worked their passage. Elitist recruitment practices pursued by the military nursing sector spilled over into the civilian field and, while the military enjoyed royal patronage for their nursing units, civilian hospitals sought to enhance their status by emphasising their own military traditions and reputations. Furthermore, by the turn of the nineteenth century the social affiliations of the nursing elite mirrored those of the military elite.

However, military influence was not confined to nursing circles during this period. Jingoistic militarism was prevalent within British society as a whole. This form of militarism was underpinned by a structural belief system that stressed the importance of the monarchy, religious values, elitism and the aristocratic tradition. In addition, the neo-feudalist stance, which emphasised the importance of character over intellect, reinforced the relationship between the civilian ruling classes and the military elite. It was this neo-feudalist stance that asserted the dictum that "nurses were born not made".

But while Nightingale had created a nursing image linked to military ideology, her system did not challenge the sexual divisions of labour and nurses remained subordinate to male physicians. Nineteenth-century nursing also incorporated middle-class notions of femininity, religious philanthropy and elements of domestic service. The emergence of militarism as the dominant force was thus associated primarily with a search for status.

Concern over nurse status was motivated not only by the desire to escape the "Mrs Gamp" image of Dickens's novels, but also to provide adequate safeguards for patients. All nurses recognised the need for official status but they failed to agree on how best to achieve this goal. Politically, nurses divided into two camps: those who followed the Nightingale line argued that status rested on the elite standing of the training hospital, while others, led by a Mrs Bedford Fenwick, pressed for state recognition by means of nurse registration.

Significantly, the drive towards registration was closely linked to the suffrage movement. War nursing in particular gave added impetus to the claims for citizenship. As Summers has argued, it was thought that "women's necessary services in war demonstrated their de facto equality with men". Ironically, though, while women viewed military nursing as a vital contribution to the war effort, male conscientious objectors within the RAMC considered war nursing in terms of participating in a life-affirming service. The 1918 Representation of the Peoples Act sent another clear message to women: by denying the vote to conscientious objectors the Act underpinned the relationship between war service and legitimate claims for citizenship.

The thirty-year battle for nurse registration was finally won in 1919, but state recognition did not lead to better or even standardised professional training schools. Politically, nurses remained fragmented and the failure to agree on policy led to government intervention and the creation of the General Nursing Council (GNC). Nursing organisations failed to assume control of curriculum developments and since registered status was not reinforced by professional standards it became increasingly vulnerable to attack. Falling recruitment figures in the interwar period indicated that young girls no longer viewed nursing as a good career option. The nursing elite had believed that registration would compensate for poor working conditions, but this assumption was not borne out by facts. Consequently, British nursing services were in a state of crisis by 1939.

MILITARISATION

There is no succinct definition of militarisation or indeed of militarism. The working definition as it applies to the nurses described in this book is provided by Martin Shaw, who maintains that during the Second World War conditions within British society produced a "particular form of warfare — welfare state". Militarism, he argues, "is not a matter of good or bad, but of how far military organisation and values (which may sometimes be justified and necessary) impinge on the social structure". Militarisation, therefore, is the process by which militarism becomes an integral part of civilian society. Within this context, nurses equated militarisation with aristocratic traditions, efficiency, class distinctions, heroic adventures and notions of a racial hierarchy constructed within an all-powerful British Empire. After all, the military had produced nurse heroines such as Florence Nightingale and Edith Cavell. Many nurses had received medals as a result of their earlier participation in war, and a large number were eager to receive similar recognition from 1939 onwards.

In view of the fact that nurses were unable to raise their professional status by any other means, it should not, therefore, be considered extraordinary that military participation and nurse status appeared once again to go hand in hand. For the registered nurse, identification with the military officer class at least offered some prestige in terms of social class. Within a society that was (and still is to some extent) based on a distinct social hierarchy, this identification with the "officer class" and its associations with the British aristocracy represented a significant prize. Even medical consultants adopted the habit of comparing civilian nurses working within individual hospitals to military regiments. Thus Sir Robert Hutchinson, a consultant at the Royal London Hospital, claimed that "Royal London nurses are like the Brigade of Guards, the pick of the Forces."

Identification with the military officer class was one thing, but the militarisation of nursing practice was another matter. The rigid military framework, especially when it was adapted to suit civilian nursing, was entirely inappropriate and prevented any flexibility in nursing practice. Even within the military there were nurses who became so obsessed by the military hierarchy that the process of treating patients according to rank assumed ludicrous proportions. For the most part, nurses and doctors in all theatres of war administered care irrespective of rank, but occasionally medical common sense appeared to desert those who administered care as the military rank structure prevailed.

But this book is not merely about nurses and war; nor just about their attempts to gain status and adequate recognition for their work. It is primarily about women, their travels, their humour, their suffering and their experiences as they related to the conditions of war. It is about how a group of highly professional women perceived themselves and their role in wartime, and how they adapted to the various social and political changes that were dictated by an international emergency. It is also the story of how civilian and military society became so intertwined that all government policies were considered in the light of how one would affect the other.

In every war in our history,
Britain has looked to the women
to care for the sick and wounded.
It is women's work.
The nurses never let us down.
Florence Nightingale lit a candle
in the Crimea 85 years ago.
The women of today
have kept it burning brightly
not only in France, Egypt and Greece
but in Poplar, Portsmouth, Liverpool, Hull
and all the other battlefields
of the Home Front.

From a Ministry of Health recruitment poster

CHAPTER ONE

Preparing for War

Throughout the 1930s, political tension in Europe increased dramatically. The rise of Hitler and the Nazi Party in Germany caused great concern. This concern was partly generated by German rearmament programmes and partly by the sinister ideological underpinning of Hitler's domestic and foreign policies. Hatred of Jews and Bolsheviks was a prominent feature of Nazi dogma, as was the desire to create a German "super-race" and to gain *Lebensraum* (living space) for the German people. According to Hitler, however, German grievances centred on the unfair territorial arrangements that had been instigated as a result of the Versailles Treaty following the First World War. Under these arrangements, the Czechoslovakia Republic had been created, albeit with a provisional government. The Republic included Czechs, Slovaks and around 3¼ million Germans. The latter were situated in what was known as the Sudetenland, an area between Silesia and Bohemia. Both British and French governments knew that, in terms of German foreign policy, Hitler wanted to reclaim the Sudetenland as part of Germany. In an attempt to appease Hitler, and hopefully to quell any further German expansionist aims, the Sudetenland was signed over to Hitler during the famous Munich agreement of September 1938.

However, when Hitler's army marched into Czechoslovakia in March 1939 it was clear that the British and French appeasement policy had been unsuccessful. The British government decided to make a diplomatic manoeuvre and signed the Anglo-Polish agreement in August 1939, which effectively stated that Britain would offer military aid to Poland should Hitler invade Polish territory. Thus the stage was set for war, and when Hitler invaded Poland on 1 September 1939, as part of his campaign to achieve *Lebensraum* in the east, Britain responded by declaring war on Germany on 3 September.

But, in theory at least, long before 1939 the British government had made substantial preparations in readiness for the outbreak of the Second World War. Thus the administrative framework for a Civil Nursing Reserve (CNR), which was to be utilised in the event of war, was firmly in place by that date; the nurses, however, were not! Poor pay, long hours and a monastic lifestyle had undermined nurse recruitment levels, and lowered morale. Consequently, the need to recruit, train and deploy nurses in adequate numbers for the duration of the war presented the government with a problem that was never fully resolved. From a government standpoint, nursing tasks were considered to be merely an extension of mothering. There was no recognition of the different levels of nurse training, nor of the technical skills that accompanied these levels. This extreme ignorance of nursing matters was reflected in government policy, and subsequently held dire consequences for both the civilian and military population. As one contemporary military observer exclaimed, "It is amazing what misconceptions are current as to the functions of the medical services in war. It is believed by quite a number of people that all that is necessary is a few doctors and nurses to bind up the wounds of casualties, with a bevy of VADs fluttering in the background."

Government officials, to an extent, based British wartime emergency schemes on medical experience that had been gained during the Spanish Civil War. But a shortage of medical personnel prevented the introduction of an efficient casualty clearance scheme. The shortage of trained nurses in particular proved to be a problem, and an official committee was appointed, chaired by the Earl of Athlone, to ascertain the disincentives to nurse recruitment. According to the Athlone Interim Report, the recruitment situation could not be improved without a substantial cash injection for voluntary hospitals. If the government agreed to subsidise these hospitals, then nurse salaries could be improved, training could be standardised, and recruitment levels would rise. The report criticised the petty discipline that was an inherent feature of nurse training and also recommended that the government afford official recognition to assistant nurses, since these women were currently administering nursing care without any official title or training.

The Athlone Interim Report was not popular in government circles, and officials opposed the idea of funding voluntary hospitals. Neither did the report gain much favour within nursing circles since it was believed that the official recognition of assistant nurses would undermine the status of registered nurses. Not surprisingly, registered nurses did not share the government view of their profession. They were anxious to prove that their nursing skills were the result of a rigorous three-year training programme and not merely the extension of some supposed maternal instinct. Furthermore, they wanted recognition of the value of these same nursing skills to the medical services overall, particularly during a state of national emergency.

With the outbreak of war the government had abandoned the minimum educational qualification for entry to nurse training in an attempt to aid recruitment, and registered nurses were understandably concerned about their status. The nursing profession had fought a thirty-year battle to obtain registration for trained nurses, before eventually achieving state recognition in 1919. Subsequently, this recognition was afforded to all nurses who endured the required three-year training period and passed the final examinations of the training school. This registration was administered by the GNC, and provided protection for the patient against charlatan nurses. But registered nurses jealously guarded their status with a tenacity that bordered on obsession. They were also keen to stress the heroic military nature of their professional history. Assistant nurses, by contrast, were those women who had not necessarily received any official training but had acquired some level of nursing expertise by way of practical experience. As nurses prepared for war conditions, the antagonism that existed between registered and assistant nurses increased, and was expressed both on the wards and in the nursing press. One disgruntled assistant nurse complained that:

> I have had 4 years' experience of medical nursing, which is the true art of nursing, in a hospital where 75 patients resided, and each case was different. I was relief nurse for 3 years and had a ward for 12 months. Following that I did $3^{1/2}$ years fever nursing at two different hospitals, one with a hundred beds, the other with 650 beds. There followed 4 full years at a very busy nursing home, medical and surgical, and lastly 4 years of private nursing. I have no certificate and no medals to show for my hard work, but I'll wager if I were to collect my testimonials they would carry me further than some of those people who are so fond of boasting about their state registered certificate and medals.

Another protested that, "Health or family reasons prevented many of us finishing our training and passing exams — not ignorance! If we had been allowed a register it would have put an end to nurses taking posts with only a few months experience behind them, and would have saved us, who have given years of service, being dubbed 'bath attendants'".

Ultimately, however, the luxury of this debate was temporarily surrendered as the chaos of war was

5

confronted. But while government and hospital administrators had initially paid little attention to the status of nurses, they were forced to rethink their attitudes as the war progressed. Nurses, meanwhile, although politically divided, viewed the war as an opportunity to improve their status: firstly, by establishing their value to the military and secondly, by expanding their spheres of nursing practice. Women overall had recognised that anything which was associated with the military and masculinity was afforded a higher status than anything that appeared to be feminine in nature. Therefore, nurses equated their skills with notions of masculine military efficiency, though not for the first time, as a Ministry of Health recruitment poster was quick to point out: "In every war in our history, Britain has looked to the women to care for the sick and wounded. It is women's work. The nurses never let us down. Florence Nightingale lit a candle in the Crimea 85 years ago. The women of today have kept it burning brightly not only in France, Egypt and Greece but in Poplar, Portsmouth, Liverpool, Hull and all the other battlefields of the Home Front." The British nursing profession clearly had a long military history, but the nursing role during the Second World War differed substantially from that of previous years. In earlier conflicts, nurses had found themselves on the frontline of battle more by accident than by design, whereas from 1939 onwards military nurses actually pursued a deliberate "frontline" policy. Moreover, as the recruitment poster suggested, the "frontline" was arbitrary, and nurses were just as likely to be killed working in London as they were in Greece. However, before looking at the different spheres of nursing in greater depth, and examining the origins and aims of the frontline policy, it is perhaps useful to describe how nurses were organised for war, and how they themselves felt about the outbreak of war.

THE NEW RECRUITS

It is fair to say that some nurses had severe qualms about entering the armed services, particularly those who had belonged to the Peace Pledge Union. Others, however, were keen to enter the fray. As Nurse Buchanan explained:

> I was on my way to a sector hospital from London because the London had made arrangements to send doctors and nurses out of London, and we were on our way to Chalkdown House in Hitchen when we heard the broadcast. We stopped on the way to the hospital just for a coffee or something and we heard the broadcast — Neville Chamberlain telling us it all. So we felt quite excited really — we almost cheered, which was terrible really when you think of it.

Some nurses, such as Monica Baly, described their enlistment process in purely practical terms: "The people who had finished their training just before the war had to find a job, as simple as that, and this offered a ready career opportunity to a whole lot of people just at that time." But there were many women and young girls who, like Kay McCormack, joined the armed forces hoping for adventure: "I decided I would join up as soon as I was qualified. I decided that the Army was perhaps a very good thing to be in. It was interesting; it had a lot of glamour to it then." Other nurses claimed that the military status and uniform was a huge attraction, particularly since civilian registered nurses were having such a difficult time protecting their position against the influx of untrained staff. As Monica asserted:

What upsets nurses more than anything I think is to be lowly regarded. The Civil Nursing Reserve on the whole was fairly lowly regarded, and the sisters in the services were highly regarded. I think the other thing of course is the uniform, undoubtedly. I mean, I went into the Air Force because I liked its uniform. If you couldn't look good in the Princess Mary Royal Air Force Nursing Service uniform you couldn't look good in anything. It was also, I might add, very expensive, and as a rather sartorial snob that rather appealed to me.

As far as the Ministry of Health was concerned, anyone who was young and fit could nurse. Inevitably, some new recruits were shocked by the reality of hospital life and the tasks that were performed by the most junior of nurses. Others were desperate to leave almost as soon as they had started. One recruit recalled her experiences as follows:

I didn't think I was going to get killed. But after a few weeks in hospital, nursing, I was so horrified at the work, and having been in sixth form at school and then having to do bedpans and spittoons, I thought I might as well get killed then I would be a heroine, you know. I really did think that — I hated it so much, but I was too proud to go home. So I thought that if I did get killed then I would be out of it and they would all be crying round the graveside. That's really true — I did feel that. The next job I was given was to go and help lay someone out. I had never seen a dead person, and they always cut the nails of people when they lay them out in hospital. I don't know if they do at home. And the nurse was cutting the nails and there was a little blood oozing. I said, "Gosh that's going to hurt when he wakes up" and she said, "When do you think that's going to be — up with St Peter, because he's dead you fool."

But if some girls were appalled by their nursing experiences, others took to the work like ducks to water, despite the rigid and petty discipline. Civilian hospitals had used the military as an example of an efficient organisation. Every hospital, and particularly the big London teaching hospitals, resembled a separate military regiment, each with its own traditions, training requirements and protocol, and each with the strict and petty discipline — an inherent feature of nurse training — of a peacetime army. This was not surprising in view of the profession's military roots, but in some hospitals the attention to detail and the military-style etiquette bordered on the obsessive. As one woman recalled:

We had mauve and white checks for the students in training with big puffed sleeves, and then long white sleeves which were detached. These white detachable sleeves had to be removed when you did anything that required you to roll up your sleeves in the ordinary way. But if you were giving meals or medicines you had to put your sleeves on, and if you talked to sister you had to put your sleeves on. If you had to bring her a message you had to quickly stop and put your sleeves on.

There were, of course, other less cumbersome rules, but it took some time for new recruits to fathom out the numerous regulations that governed every aspect of a nurse's life, including periods off duty:

The sister was always a bit of a martinet. But she kept control of her wards, and her wards ran like clockwork. We grumbled about her — we were only young girls — but looking back I can see she was very fair, but if there was any sliding of discipline you were really for it. To begin with I think I had one day off a month, and quite often was told the day before when the day off was to be, and certainly for our daily off-duty we were told in the morning. We went on at 7a.m. and had to get everything spick and span for sister at 8.30a.m. She said ward prayers and afterwards we all lined up and she said, "Now you can be off this morning nurse, and you can be off this afternoon." So you rushed to see if your friends had the same luck or misfortune. The matron used to do a ward round every morning on every ward, and she wore white gloves, and she would go round all the ledges with her white gloves, every morning. And she would go round and inspect all the sluices because we were responsible for the sluices and bathrooms. You were hauled up before her if she found anything untoward that you were responsible for because we all had our own jobs.

Not surprisingly, this rigid system of discipline deterred nurse recruitment at a time when hospitals needed all the girls they could lay their hands on. There was a considerable demand for women to work in the munitions factories and on the land, and these other fields of employment offered women better pay and shorter hours. Eventually, the nursing profession realised that the only way they could compete was by employing girls straight from school, before they had been given a chance to experience these better conditions. Consequently, the profession instigated pre-nursing courses in schools and established military-style "cadet schemes" to encourage girls to enter the profession at an early age, and to "obviate the tragic wastage of ability that occurs between the school leaving age and the entrance into hospital". This policy did yield fruit, in that girls from the age of fifteen upwards flocked into preliminary training courses and nurse cadet schemes. The policy did not, however, resolve the problems that were associated with a shortage of trained nurses, nor did it aid recruitment to the CNR.

THE CIVIL NURSING RESERVE

The CNR was considered to be an essential component of the wartime emergency services. The Ministry of Health had outlined a system of first-aid posts with the intention that all such posts would be staffed by a qualified doctor with trained nurses in attendance. Voluntary hospitals in the cities were to act as casualty clearing stations, and plans were unveiled to disperse large sections of the population living in the major cities to surrounding rural areas. The government also introduced an Emergency Hospital scheme, which divided the country into sectors with a matron and administrative staff for each sector. From the outset, however, there were fundamental problems associated with the emergency medical services, and more particularly with the CNR. To begin with there were not enough doctors and nurses to staff the first-aid posts. Then there was the problem of medical specialism. Doctors who were available were not necessarily experienced in orthopaedic surgery, and many did not possess the medical skills that were required to deal with air-raid casualties.

Clearly the health care needs of the civilian population were to be subordinated to those of the emergency services for the duration of the war. As the Minister of Health, Walter Elliot, announced to the nursing press in August 1939:

On the development of an emergency the government would ask every hospital in the country to send home as many patients as were fit to go, provided that their homes were not in areas to be evacuated. This would dispose of 30-50 per cent of the normal occupants of the hospitals. Those who could not be returned home would be evacuated by ambulance and ambulance train to hospitals in the outer areas. The accommodation of these hospitals is to be increased by setting up extra beds in wards and ancillary buildings. The Ministry of Health estimate that in this way approximately 300,000 beds could be made available for casualties in England and Wales. Of these over half would be first-class surgical beds and the remainder would be suitable for medical and convalescent cases.

In addition, the Ministry claimed that over 100,000 bedsteads and mattresses, 220,000 stretchers, 500,000 blankets and 200,000 pillows had already been ordered and distributed.

What Walter Elliot failed to point out was that many of the patients who were to be ousted from their hospital beds were suffering from long-term diseases such as tuberculosis and thus needed to be isolated from the wider community. As a direct result of this policy, Britain subsequently experienced a tuberculosis epidemic. The Minister also failed to admit that nearly all first-aid posts were to be staffed by inexperienced personnel, some with less than three weeks' training. Attempts to recruit nurses to the CNR had failed dismally, partly because of poor organisation, bungling and red tape, and partly because the Ministry of Health did not outline the terms and conditions of service until August 1939. Naturally, girls were not willing to commit themselves to an unknown quantity, and many were keen to do other forms of war work. Things did not improve once the conditions were announced; in fact, there was total mayhem. The Ministry stated that registered nurses working with the CNR would be paid £90 per annum, whereas the average pay for a registered nurse working in a hospital at this time was £70 per annum. As a result of these salary discrepancies, hundreds of hospital nurses left their permanent posts to join the CNR. The ensuing state of confusion brought the nursing services to the brink of collapse.

Nevertheless, for the most part, the CNR consisted of assistant nurses and auxiliaries rather than registered nurses, and initially was confined to working with the emergency services. Thus registered nurses who had left their civilian employment to join the armed forces were usually replaced by assistant nurses, although sometimes this dilution of trained personnel constituted a deliberate attempt on the part of hospitals to disregard the importance of nurse registration and to use wartime conditions as an excuse to reduce their wage bills. Consequently, thousands of registered nurses were made redundant in cities all over the country. The deployment of the CNR, therefore, had undermined registered nurse status and suggested to the public at large that anyone with a few days' training could claim the title "nurse". The same was true of the deployment of Voluntary Aid Detachment (VAD) nurses.

VOLUNTARY AID DETACHMENT NURSES

VAD nurses were recruited and trained by the British Red Cross and the Order of St John. They were better organised than the nurses of the CNR and, in some cases, better trained. The VAD scheme generally was designed to supplement the military and civilian medical services in the event of a national emergency and consisted of trained and untrained personnel from most medical fields. Most VAD nurses had received at least twelve lectures on first aid and a minimum of fifty hours' practical nursing experience in a hospital. The tasks performed by VAD nurses were stipulated by the VAD Council, and this body also regulated their hours of work and conditions of employment. However, due to the shortage of nurses, inexperienced VADs were often found staffing the first-aid posts and casualty clearing stations. Two days before the outbreak of war, the government's Central Emergency Committee issued an urgent appeal for more women to come forward and join the nursing services, and stated that, "those nurses who have completed their first-aid and nursing lectures will be allocated to duties even if they lack the compulsory fifty to ninety hours' practical hospital training". Further, that, "Every nurse single or married should feel it her duty to volunteer for some form of nursing service, so that the country may have the benefit of their expert knowledge. It is to the retired or married nurse that our appeal is specially directed."

Before 1939 most women were required to give up their employment on marriage, and it was therefore particularly significant that the government was now

15

appealing directly to married women to help with the war effort. It was estimated that 9,700 volunteers had enrolled as VAD nurses by 1 September, but only a small proportion of these were registered. In addition to the registered nurses, assistants and auxiliaries, 3,400 partially trained women enrolled as volunteers. These were women who had undergone some form of training but either had not taken nursing exams or, in some instances, had not passed them. Subsequently, the British Red Cross and the Order of St John attempted to make a cohesive nursing service from what was essentially a very motley crew. Among other things, the new recruits were given a manual to guide them through the mysteries of hospital etiquette. As the following extracts reveal, a junior needed to pay considerable attention to the levels of authority:

The matron — is the supreme authority for the junior probationer in hospital, and will be looked upon by her in very much the same light as was her headmistress during school days. A nurse is directly responsible to the sister in charge of the department in which she is working, and the sister is responsible to the matron, so that in the ordinary course of events a junior nurse will approach matron through the sister, though most matrons are always ready to help and advise the nurse should the nurse go to her with any difficulty with which the sister cannot deal. Should the matron enter a ward or department in which the sister is not immediately available, it is the business of any nurse who happens to be at hand, however junior, to go to her and offer her services to find sister or a senior nurse, or to do anything the matron may require of her.

The sisters — a certain respect, implicit obedience and loyalty are due to everyone in positions of authority in hospitals by reason of their added experience. The same courtesy should be shown to the sisters and senior sisters as is accorded to one's own parents at home.

The medical staff — at home, the doctor in charge of the case may have been an old family friend and the nurse's relations with him one of the friendliest, but in hospital professional etiquette demands a very different relationship between the nurse and the medical staff. It is extremely unlikely that any communications will pass between a probationer nurse and a medical man on the wards. Anything regarding the patient's condition which the doctor needs to know will be told him by the sister or senior nurse in charge, and should an emergency arise while sister is with the doctor, any communication should be made to the sister who will inform the doctor if necessary. A nurse will never inform the doctor of anything of which the sister, if on duty, is not already aware.

Armed with the knowledge gleaned from a few lectures and very little practical experience most VADs launched themselves into the war with enthusiasm. They were, however, brought down with a bump as many of them realised the conditions under which they were expected to live and the tasks they were supposed to perform. The VAD Council was overwhelmed with complaints from VADs almost as soon as they went on duty. Some of these complaints centred on the substandard accommodation that was offered to the VAD nurses by the armed forces. The remainder were concerned with individual nursing tasks. Many VADs objected to menial work and believed that the basic and more unsavoury aspects of nursing care should be the preserve of the RAMC orderlies. In an attempt to pacify the VAD Council, the Army Council limited the scope of VAD duties and afforded them officer privileges. But although these concessions were offered in good faith, they merely fuelled existing levels of discontent. Qualified nurses resented the fact that VAD nursing assistants were afforded officer privileges. Qualified non-nursing VADs such as opticians and radiographers were disappointed because they were denied these same privileges, and male RAMC orderlies expressed considerable dissatisfaction because they were now expected to perform all the unskilled nursing tasks.

This level of discontent among military nursing grades escalated rapidly as it was realised that although VADs had been awarded officer privileges, they were clearly unable to assume officer workloads; neither could these same VADs adequately replace RAMC orderlies. Moreover, the problems associated with VAD task allocation were likely to affect strategic medical plans. How was the Army expected to move medical units near to the frontline if VADs could not replace registered nurses and RAMC orderlies back at the base hospitals? The military nursing services had formed their own reserve forces in preparation for war, but even so, the armed forces were expected to sustain substantial casualties. Efficient medical planning was, therefore, vital to ensure the ultimate success of military campaigns.

THE MILITARY NURSING SERVICES

The military nursing services possessed a history that dated back to the Crimean War, and were considered to be the nursing elite. As the official history of the Royal College of Nursing (RCN) acknowledged: "Naturally only girls and women who were dedicated to nursing would endure conditions which were exacerbated by a tradition of constant bullying and purposeful fault-finding by the sisters. This had its parallel in the ranks of the Regular Army, and it was upon Army traditions and customs that Florence Nightingale had founded skilled nursing." As the nursing elite, military nurses were even more aware of their status than their colleagues working in the civilian field. The military nursing services were the only female units to be retained by the forces at the end of the First World War, and had been afforded nominal officer status since the Crimean War. However, this status was based purely on social class. Military nurses were recruited primarily from the ranks of officers' wives, widows and daughters, and this elitist recruitment practice, combined with royal patronage, ensured that the military nursing services occupied a prestigious position within the profession overall. They had also adopted the aristocratic military view that a person's "character was more important than their intellect" (military nurses, therefore, were born not made).

Despite this prestige, though, the position of nurses within the forces was always ambiguous. Furthermore, with the onset of war this position was threatened by the arrival of female military units such as the Auxiliary Territorial Service (ATS). Certainly, in terms of pay and status, women working in military nursing compared unfavourably with the women working in the ATS, and appeared to be less valued. They were also supposed to be "sexless" when administering care to patients as one nurse recalled: "All the services wore these little capes and you know what the tippets were for. It was to hide your sex appeal really. And we were asked if we knew why we wore the tippets, by the regular matrons, and that was the official answer. That you are always in command and always being respected."

In an attempt to protect their status, the military nursing services refused to take on any regulars during the course of the war. Consequently, they were far outnumbered by reserve nurses. The Queen Alexandra's Imperial Military Nursing Service (QAIMNS, Army) expanded from 624 to 12,000, the Queen Alexandra's Royal Naval Nursing Service (QARNNS, Navy) from 78 to 1,341, and the Princess Mary's Royal Air Force Nursing Service (PMRAFNS Air Force) from 171 to a total of 1,215 members. Regular military nurses received their initial registration training in civilian hospitals before entering the service environment, where the recruitment procedures were extremely selective. Thus one justification for the strict discipline meted out to trainee civilian nurses was the general acceptance that some of these nurses would eventually be subjected to military discipline.

However, the belief that the military nursing services were more efficient and better organised than the civilian nursing services was completely unfounded. On the eve of war, military nurses were just as confused as their civilian counterparts. One QA nurse describes the level of chaos: "I had secret orders, and my orders were to report to Netley Hospital which is outside Southampton. It was an absolute shambles really and it wasn't very well organised. We arrived there to find that the Matron of Netley had to report to Colchester hospital, and the assistant matron had to report somewhere else, and here were all of us not knowing anything about Army matters at all."

The organisation of all the nursing services left a lot to be desired, but there was at least an attempt to prepare military nurses for frontline service, as one nurse explained:

The Hydro itself, where we had the hospital, was not busy then but we had a most invigorating course of instruction from the Regimental Sergeant Major who hadn't much time for sisters. He thought we would be a bit of an encumbrance when the hospital did move, so he took us up hill and down dale carrying our rucksacks and as much heavy material as he could drum up for us. We didn't work out awfully well at first and we puffed and blew. But he showed us how to put a tent up, with demonstrations on the tennis courts, and this peacetime hotel was really transformed into a hive of activity.

As military nurses prepared for the frontline, most were unaware that their frontline service would be crucial to the success of a distinct militarisation strategy. The Matron-in-Chief of the Army, Dame Katherine Jones, was intent on gaining commissioned officer status for her registered nurses and believed that the only way to achieve this goal was for nurses to be viewed as soldiers first and nurses second. As she herself asserted:

The ATS achieved that understanding from the start. It was recognised by a multitude of detailed practices, it was emphasised by the cut and the colour of her uniform and there was no doubt at any point that she fitted into the army pattern. She was recognised everywhere by everyone as an army officer both on and off duty. It became my aim to profit from this experience and to achieve the same assimilation for the QAIMNS.

Dame Katherine also believed that if registered nurses in the military sector obtained commissioned officer status this would have a "knock on" effect in the civilian nursing sector, thus elevating nurse status overall. "I want you to understand this as the imposition of the military rank pattern on the nursing profession. By superimposing this rank pattern on one particular section of the nursing profession, it seemed possible to not only confer status but to provide a framework to hold that status firmly in place."

The process of military assimilation ensured that all military nurses were subjected to fitness programmes. In addition to the "aristocratic" military view about the importance of character, they were also expected to adopt the concept of technocratic military efficiency and to suppress the more feminine aspects of nursing care. Battledress was eventually introduced, and nurses began to administer care in frontline positions. The latter policy formed the basis of Dame Katherine's overall militarisation strategy, but it was one that provoked a good deal of controversy among male military officers. There were those who argued that nurses should be present in operational areas, since their presence might be good for the morale of the troops. Others, though, believed that nurses should remain in base hospitals, and argued that their presence in operational areas might compromise military activity and confuse evacuation procedures.

However, just like the status arguments that centred on assistant nurses in the civilian sector and VADs in the military sector, the controversy over whether or not women should be allowed to work in the frontline of battle gave way to the initial demands of war. These same arguments were to be resurrected as the war progressed. But, for a while at least, the immediate chaos took precedence over petty squabbles and gender issues. Since all the nursing and medical services were diluted with untrained personnel almost as soon as war was declared, the outbreak of war in 1939 was accompanied by an outbreak of confusion in the British nursing services. The outpatient departments of city hospitals disappeared virtually overnight, and their existing inpatients were evacuated to rural areas. This process placed a severe burden on the district nursing service. Moreover, because a substantial number of registered nurses had flocked into the armed forces, the civilian nursing services were severely depleted. It was not long, therefore, before Britain's nursing services were on the verge of a total breakdown.

CHAPTER
TWO

Chaos on the Home Front

By the end of September 1939 there were at least 30,000 women in the CNR, but only 7,000 of these were registered nurses. The remainder consisted of approximately 3,000 assistant nurses and 20,000 auxiliaries. Luckily for those girls who did not know the difference between a heart attack and a hernia, Britain was, for the first few months, suspended in a state of "phoney war". The regular civilian nursing services were severely understaffed, particularly in areas that dealt with mental health, chronic illnesses such as tuberculosis, and midwifery. But despite these shortages the government initially refused to supplement these nursing fields with CNR nurses. Thus the ludicrous situation arose whereby the CNR nurses spent their time idly bandaging chair legs, waiting for the arrival of casualties who never materialised, while nurses who were working in the sanatoriums were continually rushed off their feet. This situation, combined with a dire shortage of registered nurses, salary discrepancies between regular and reserve nurses, and an ad hoc scheme for training new recruits, was a formula for total chaos.

THE PHONEY WAR

Although by the beginning of March 1940 the CNR had expanded to include 40,000 members, many of these women abandoned the reserve during the latter part of the "phoney war". Most were bored by the lack of work and sought alternative employment. The government had envisaged a large mobile CNR, able to move at a moment's notice and able to cope with any emergency. Instead, it had managed to establish a group of women, some unsuitable from the outset, with only a half-hearted interest in nursing. Many could not even begin to be mobile because they were restricted by domestic obligations. CNR nurses were usually allocated to first-aid posts, evacuation trains, wartime nurseries and to hospitals designated for the reception of wartime casualties. But some were only attached to the CNR on a part-time basis and their training at best had been sporadic, and at worst, non-existent.

Government propaganda insisted that the medical services were in a constant state of readiness and prepared for any emergency. However, this same propaganda was always careful to refer to first-aiders as "personnel" rather than as trained nurses or first-aiders, since first-aid posts were usually staffed by inexperienced volunteers. But despite the fact that these first-aid posts could not claim to be in a constant state of readiness for all emergencies, most were reasonably equipped to deal with minor injuries. The primary function of such posts was to prevent hospitals from becoming blocked with minor casualties. As such, they were designed to provide care for the walking wounded and bomb victims who had sustained minor injuries. However, since trained nurses were not available to staff such posts, there was no valid criteria for assessing the seriousness of individual injuries. In the event, most volunteers believed that it was "better to be safe than sorry", and sent many casualties to hospital unnecessarily, thus defeating the purpose of the first-aid posts.

The civilian inpatients of city hospitals were evacuated to rural areas and were generally attached to mental institutions or workhouses. For the nurses working in these sector hospitals the change was dramatic:

It was quite an experience because Chopdale was a workhouse, and they had cleared the Infirmary where the inmates would normally go if they were ill. They had put all the old people into strange wards and had cleared this building for us to prepare for casualties, which for a year we didn't get. We were horrified really because we found that the people who were there were unmarried mothers or fallen girls, the poor, the elderly and tramps. There were tramps' wards, casual wards and there were cells for drunks who could be picked up and put there. But the building we were in was reasonable.

We spent Christmas there. The matron of this workhouse wanted to give us a nice Christmas Day and we had quite a nice first course. Then the Christmas pudding was brought in, aflame, how marvellous. We said, "how lovely", Christmas pudding and we all tackled it, and we discovered that it had been set alight by methylated spirits — which was awful. But we felt that we had had Christmas Day in the workhouse!

In addition to the general problems that emerged as a result of changing circumstances, there were also difficulties associated with nurse training. A nurse from the Royal London Hospital wrote the following in the nurses' review:

In some cases the units were left entirely alone, in others they were just added to the present staff of the hospital. This arrangement was not so satisfactory, because their methods of administration were so different from our own. As a result it became very difficult to carry on with the training of our nurses, as so often they were not working under London Hospital Sisters, but, of course, that like everything else, had to be overlooked until the initial emergency was over.

The initial emergency, however, was merely the calm before the storm and many people described the "phoney war" as a "war of nerves". Indeed, there were numerous medical lectures throughout the war, such as those given by Dr Henry Wilson, psychiatrist to the London Hospital, which debated whether or not the British personality was equipped to withstand the bombing and mass destruction. Dr Wilson claimed that the way an individual reacted to war depended entirely on the personality type of that individual before the war began:

The problem of wartime nerves is the individual's problem of reaction. Is he going to isolate himself from others and act in a childlike way, dependent, crying out for help to other people, asking others to make the decisions, complaining of this or that, or is he going to allow his own feelings to be merged into those of the group of which he forms a body? In other words, is he going to be a self-isolator or a self-liquidator? Is he going to recognise responsibility to himself alone, like the persons with panic who forget about their family, or is he to say, in the acute danger through which I am living here is an opportunity of helping others and helping the community in which I live?

Dr Wilson also highlighted the paranoia that appeared to be a longstanding feature of wartime nerves, stating that, "there was a porter or coalman — anyway, one of the artisan staff — and he began to make insinuations against the matron. When asked what he meant, he said he was quite certain matron was causing the washing to be hung out on the roof to help the enemy."

The Ministry of Health was also bitten by the paranoia bug. Nurses from countries other than Britain had been nursing in hospitals all over the country before the outbreak of war, but suddenly these nurses found themselves labelled as "aliens". Instructions were issued to all hospitals to restrict the areas where these alien nurses were allowed to work. They were not allowed to nurse on male wards or come into contact with any members of the armed forces. There were matrons who flouted these instructions, however, partly because some alien nurses were in training — and matrons insisted that experience of working on male wards was an essential part of that training — and partly because staff shortages dictated that alien nurses worked in any area where they were needed.

Government posters with cartoon drawings of Hitler hiding behind trees and innocent people on buses and captions stating that "careless talk costs lives" did nothing to help this wartime paranoia. But the British personality was about to be put to the test. In April 1940 Britain was defeated in its Norwegian campaign, and Neville Chamberlain resigned as prime minister. Winston Churchill took over, and the following month Germany invaded Holland. By the end of June Belgium, the Netherlands and France were occupied by German forces. The "phoney war" was over and the Blitz began. From September 1940 to May 1941 the German Luftwaffe subjected major British cities and ports to unremitting waves of aerial bombardment. More than 50 per cent of all the civilian casualties of the war (over 80,000) were sustained during this period, and it was some testimony to the British personality that when Gallup opinion polls were conducted early in 1941, most people claimed that they were more depressed by the British weather than by Hitler's bombs. In fact, people seemed to be more disturbed by the "flying bomb" doodlebug attacks of 1944 than they were by this earlier Blitz period.

NURSING IN THE BLITZ

The Blitz began at a time when 90 per cent of evacuee adults and children had returned to the cities. Many had been unhappy in the reception areas and were lulled into a false sense of security by the "phoney war". Some arrived just in time for the bombing, as Dame Kathleen Raven recalled:

In August a few bombs were dropped on the city, but it was not until September the 7th that we experienced the whole fury and might of the enemy. At 5p.m., I remember it was still daylight, waves of German bombers dropped their bombs on the city and the docks and the East End. Casualties were coming in, the whole sky was like a great red sunset in the wrong place — in the east — and this immense vivid red light guided the next onslaught which came at 7p.m. Barts was hit that night. I was caring for casualties on the first floor of the new block when I was blown right across the ward, the blast taking the window and all before it, I was unhurt.

Hundreds of casualties were brought to us that night, the theatres worked non-stop and the nurses and doctors worked together day and night. We patched up the charred and broken bodies and as soon as they were fit to move we saw them off to Hill End on the Green Line ambulances — to prepare the beds for the next onslaught.

By this time the underground stations were being used as air-raid shelters, and every evening if one happened to venture outside, one could witness queues of people with some bedding waiting to buy a 1½d ticket for the tube where they spent the night. As the war proceeded, chalk or paint marks were made on the platforms allotting space to the families and the electricity on the tubes was cut, so that more people could shelter underground on the actual rails and in the tunnels and even on the stationary escalators. It was a sight never to be forgotten.

Large numbers of people viewed the London underground stations as natural air-raid shelters, and the Red Cross and other charitable organisations frequently entertained the people as they lay huddled together for safety and warmth. There were even instances when midwives were called to the underground to deliver babies. Nevertheless, the underground stations were not always the safest place to take refuge, as Dame Kathleen explained:

I think one of the worst nights for us, as regards pain, sorrow and death, was when bombs blasted through the Bank underground stations, carrying the flaming debris right down to the platforms and burying the people taking refuge there, and burning them so as to be unrecognisable. Many, many casualties were brought to us that night and I have never seen such burns in my life — black charred bodies, still alive. We had to do our best. Nurses performed things in 1940 that were unheard of previously.

Most of this nursing care was administered by junior nurses, and some were as young as fifteen. These girls had joined the profession straight from school as "cadets", and were understandably daunted by the array of appalling injuries with which they were confronted day after day. They quickly adapted to the furious pace of work, but like all nurses, they were expected to suppress their own feelings of fear in an attempt to instil courage in their patients. With this aim in mind, the majority of nurses carried on their work as normal, and gave their patients the appearance that all was well with the world:

People often ask me what I felt like during my first experience of bombing when I was on duty. Well, to tell the truth, I felt as though it wasn't real. There was an awful din going on but there was work to be done and someone had to do it, and there was nothing exciting to tell. Working at night during the blitz was not as terrifying as you might think. Knowing that other people are depending on you helps you to forget your fear. Often when my knees have gone to jelly, the patients think I am calm and cheerful. If only they could hear the racket my heart is making.

There was bombing because we used to have to wheel the patients out of the wards in their beds into the main corridor because there were no windows in that, you see, so the windows could not blow in on them. There was sticking paper all over the windows, they did that in a criss cross pattern.

* * *

We had casualties in. We had one dear old lady come in, I remember, from Peabody buildings in Hammersmith. She was very very dirty, a sweet old soul, but she was dirty and smelt dreadful. She had a terrific gash on her leg. I had to get her clothes off and she apologised in a broad cockney accent, "I'm sorry luv, I haven't had my bath this week, but I have washed up as far as possible and I've washed down as far as possible." I remember the casualty doctor saying, "I wish she had washed possible sometimes because she did smell absolutely dreadful."

It was the first night Southampton was bombed. We had one patient who had been delivered — a maternity case — and there was another one in labour. One of my CCS staff had come down to see me for the night. She was awaiting posting orders. So we moved the patient who had had the baby under the bed, on the two bedded ward, and I delivered the woman, who was a staff sergeant RAMC's wife, at about 2.15 in the morning, with a hurricane lamp held by Sister Wood. We put a steel helmet on the mother — what for I don't know — but I delivered her safely of a baby boy at about 2.30 in the morning while the bombs were raining down on Southampton.

Another nurse, Iris Bower, recalled her experiences of nursing in the Blitz as follows:

I was a junior sister at the time, but it so happened on this particular night, I had been detailed to be in charge in the absence of the senior sister. I was making one of my routine rounds of the hospital with an experienced VAD. She was one of those wonderful Red Cross nurses who contributed so much during the war years. Patients in service hospitals appreciated their dedication and kindness. Suddenly we heard bombs dropping with no warning at all, they had beaten the siren to it. It seemed an eternity before the siren started wailing in the darkness. I heard Nurse Traherne shouting, "Don't run!" In a few seconds I had reached a ward full of patients and found the entrance vanished. It was pitch black, shouting, moaning and rushing water could be heard. Suddenly, I seemed to be falling into a deep hole and realized it was a bomb crater. I climbed out pretty fast, and the first patient I came to was still sitting on the lavatory seat, all the walls had disappeared. I could see by the light of my torch that blood was streaming down his face. He was shocked but by some miracle not badly hurt. In no time at all, we could see the funny side to the situation that he was still sitting on the loo!

We groped our way in the darkness and seemed to be wading through water before reaching some of the other patients who were injured and in obvious pain. Fortunately, most had minor injuries, only due to the fact that the wards were wooden huts and there was no heavy masonry. The most menacing sound in the darkness was that of rushing water, as all the pipes had been fractured. In no time at all help was on hand. Doctors, nurses and medical orderlies descended upon us and the task of moving patients began. Some were moved temporarily to an underground shelter and others evacuated immediately to the Royal Infirmary, Cardiff. The ghostly figures running about and the ambulances coming and going made it a hectic night, still vivid in my mind. The medical staff worked tirelessly with great efficiency and there was a great deal of courage amongst the patients. We were all glad to see the dawn.

The Palace Hotel had been taken over by the RAF for use as a hospital. About this time, "Lord Haw Haw", in one of his propaganda broadcasts, had threatened that there would be a reprisal. He claimed that the RAF had bombed some hospital or convalescent home in Germany. On this Sunday morning I was walking along the first floor of the hotel, where the operating theatre was, and all the surgical cases. With me was a very young, delightful and pretty Australian VAD. She was affectionately known, to all the staff and patients, as "Tinkerbell". At that moment, a medical officer spoke to me, asked me to accompany him to see four patients in a nearby room. I told the VAD that I would join her as soon as I could. The MO and myself walked into the room and at that moment we both saw, through the large windows, German planes, with their swastikas clearly visible. There was no time to be brave or heroic, we dived under the bed and heard the unforgettable sound of bombs dropping.

They had dropped without warning from the clear skies. I later learned that four low flying Fw 190s had approached the hotel from the sea. Although there had been several explosions, which had missed the hotel, one was a direct hit. The four patients, the doctor and myself were in one piece, but the door and windows of the room were out. An Australian pilot in the bed by the window, who had his leg in traction, was covered in broken glass, but mercifully was not badly injured. We hurried out of the room to find just dust and rubble everywhere and, where there had been a further room, just one big gaping hole. We looked to the right, where I was originally making for, and were filled with horror, just rubble and clouds of dust.

The first body we came to was that of "Tinkerbell". I saw her hand and arm with its frilled cuff sticking out beneath the heavy masonry. I also saw the incredible sight of two bodies which seemed to be hanging from the girder. The bomb had gone through all the floors down to the basement. The whole wing had collapsed. Many patients and staff were killed. Some had miraculous escapes, like myself, and some ended in tragedy. One young pilot, who had gone to a waiting taxi just before the bombing, returned to his room to collect something and was killed. If it had not been a Sunday the casualties would have been even higher. Some of the patients, who were at the stage of rehabilitation, fractured spines in plaster casts, etc., would normally have been in the basement.

It was a devastating and horrific experience. Many, who had been badly injured, received some immediate treatment, including blood transfusions, in the part of the building that was more or less intact. We were all rushing about and I remember nuns appearing from somewhere assisting with the casualties, one in particular, comforting a Group Captain who was one of my surgical patients, but as a result of the bombing had additional serious injuries. All the injured were soon evacuated to other hospitals. Like many of the nursing staff, I accepted the hospitality of a Torquay family and slept the night in their home.

The following morning we were on our way by coach to RAF Hospital, Wroughton, in Wiltshire. I think it took us several days to feel normal. I had the strange unnerving experience of feeling the closeness of the little VAD "Tinkerbell". Her presence was with me everywhere I went for about three days, then it seemed to leave me suddenly. I have never in my life experienced such a feeling. It was almost frightening.

Life for nurses working outside hospitals was no less fraught. A wartime nursing auxiliary, Rhoda Evans, described her life on the number seven ambulance train.

In the station was a long train made up of cattle trucks with gutters down the middle of the floors. Commands were given and the long seats on the platforms were man-handled into the coaches. All the newspapers on a kiosk were taken for use on the train. Then we were paired off with a sister. Three of the sisters had been in the First World War. Two had been sent to Siberia and Sister Barker, who seemed to be in charge had served on the frontline in France.

Soon the patients from Hallam hospital began to arrive; stretcher cases, others in chairs and some walking. Sister and I had the ward with the latter and a small boy who sat on a pile of newspapers looking through a hole at the passing scene. He had never been on a train before.

After the journey we ate our sandwiches. Then Sister Barker called for volunteers to shake, fold and count the blankets we had received in exchange for ours. This had to be done after every journey. We returned home very tired indeed.

Next we had to report to Monument Road Station. In the sheds we found a dirty banana train which had to be scrubbed and scraped clean. We were issued with giant-sized operating gowns to protect our clothing. They had to be tucked up and in by a piece of bandage round our waists. When the train was clean we were issued with our uniforms — skirts to be worn 12 inches above the ground. Thank goodness I was stock size — others had to do a lot of altering. The train was sent to Derby for fitting out and painting and we were packed off to Queens (Birmingham Accident Hospital) for a while. We were promptly nicknamed the milkmaids because our caps were made of white cloth and a short length of elastic with holes in!

When the train returned we started our journeys again, moving people from London and the east coast to safer places. Once we travelled overnight to Great Yarmouth. At Peterborough we stopped at 3.30a.m. and were given strawberries by men lined up with their goods for market. Soon we saw the sun rise like a great golden ball straight out of the ground. A hospital was closing and we took on their very good chef and three orderlies. Some of the patients were sedated but one on our ward came round and began to struggle with the other younger nurse. I held her — she was very thin but very strong. Nurse ran for the doctor who came armed with a huge syringe and calm was restored.

Sometimes an enemy plane would pick us up and begin passing back and forth over us. Our speed would be reduced to four miles an hour as we were a harder target to hit at that speed. We did look rather like an ammunition train but supposedly had red crosses on the roof.

We usually picked up our patients at Watford junction but on one occasion went into London to get some Jews. There were bomb craters alongside the line and the ambulances bringing the patients had been machine-gunned. The Church Army gave us sandwiches and tea. The Jews seemed to have all their possessions with them. Some even had two fur coats and many had rings with real gems. Some were very orthodox and would not eat the food we had prepared for them, even though our doctor was a Jew.

Every journey was different and I enjoyed them, but I got fed up with the endless dusting and shaking of blankets between whiles. Doctor was also fed up at times (he even learnt to knit!). He did give us some interesting talks on diagnosing and we did practical things like giving injections and bandaging. To break the monotony we opened Monument Lane baths [sic] and went to see *Gone with the Wind*.

One dark, damp foggy night during the blackout of 1940 we decided to cross the lines to reach our train, stabled in Powell's Wood goods yard. We edged our way forward, slowly and sightlessly in the inky black. Then Whoosh! A blacked-out express rushed past on its way to New Street. Another two feet forward and we would have been patients ourselves.

On another occasion we were involved in the bombing of Kent Street. Having dug out three casualties and taken them to the First Aid Post, we found it had just been bombed. Sister seemed shell shocked — the nurses who had been either side of her had been blown away; two more on the stairs had been stripped naked. My dad and another man ran to get blankets to cover them. They would not let us downstairs to help even though I was in uniform and the others were first aiders. All sister wanted was a cup of tea. She looked at me as if I were a ghost, perhaps one of her nurses who had run to the next aid post to telephone for help. I saw two nurses amongst the rubble, one was bleeding and made a little movement and groaned. I bathed her face with water from one of the buckets that stood there, to stop the blood going into her eyes and mouth. I had never really smelt blood before. Three men with a stretcher came running through and kicked the water all over us. As I was soaked and thought they had come to collect the patients, I went home.

Clearly nurses of all grades were doing their best to administer an adequate standard of care to all their patients despite increasingly difficult working conditions. In some instances they were even expanding their spheres of influence. There was much rejoicing among the members of the nursing profession when hospitals, admittedly through a lack of male staff, decided that nurses should be allowed to run the operating theatres. As Miss Littleboy exclaimed in the *Nurses' League Review* of the London hospital, "On March the 1st the theatres were taken over by me and are now entirely run by the nursing staff. (Applause.) This, as you will realise has meant a lot of reorganisation and it will take some time before they are running exactly as we would wish. This, however, will mean that far more nurses can have theatre experience than was possible in the past."

This rejoicing, however, was short-lived. The whole of the civilian nursing sector had been significantly diluted with untrained personnel, and there were numerous instances of dangerous and neglectful nursing practices. Inexperienced nurses were a liability, but they were often in positions of responsibility because other more skilled nurses had left the civilian sector to join the armed forces. One young girl, "when counting the swabs at an orthopaedic operation said that the number was correct even though she knew she had recounted and there was one missing. Later she said that she did this for 'peace and happiness' as the surgeon was getting irritable." This incident was by no means the only one of its kind. Hospitals all over the country were suffering the loss of senior nursing staff caused by the unrestricted flow of nurses into the forces. The disjointed CNR only compounded the problem. In addition, shortages in the midwifery, psychiatric and sanatorium nursing fields were causing concern, and by 1941 the civilian nursing services were on the point of collapse. Ministry of Health officials were forced to admit that their overall concern had been for quantity of nurses not quality. Belatedly, these officials asked for nursing advice.

NURSES ENTER WHITEHALL

In an attempt to resolve the nursing crisis the government created three chief nursing officer posts at Whitehall: the first at the Ministry of Health, the second at the Ministry of Labour, and the third at the Colonial Office. Along with the Matron-in-Chief at the War Office, these nursing officers were expected to lick the nursing services into shape for the remainder of the war. In 1941 it was the civilian nursing services that demanded the most attention. The health of the civilian population was suffering as a result of the nursing shortages and urgent action was needed to prevent a further deterioration. The newly appointed nursing officers urged the government to adopt a three-pronged approach to improve the situation. Consequently, the role of the CNR was no longer restricted to the emergency services but extended to include all nursing fields. In addition, steps were taken by the War Office to return senior nurses to their respective hospitals on request, if the institutions concerned were experiencing difficulties in filling senior positions. Finally, the Ministry of Health insisted that all hospitals paid their own nurses at the same rate as nurses working for the CNR.

These measures had a limited effect on the nursing situation. The extension of the CNR role improved staffing levels in most general hospitals, but the sanatoriums and mental institutions remained understaffed. Most CNR nurses did not want to nurse in the sanatoriums in case they actually caught tuberculosis. Mental nursing was considered to be more of a man's job, since before the widespread use of tranquillisers psychiatric patients frequently needed to be physically restrained. Recruitment to the sanatorium and mental hospitals was also hampered by the fact that these institutions were usually situated in isolated places. Some nurses did not have the necessary means of transport to travel to and from work, and did not want to live in hospital accommodation for fear of becoming isolated themselves.

The steps taken by the War Office to return senior nurses to their respective hospitals were largely ineffective. The time lapse between making a request to the War Office and receiving the released nurse tended to be a period of at least six months because senior nurses who had joined the armed forces were often overseas. It was, therefore, virtually impossible to locate and return these nurses to their civilian hospitals. Government intervention in the CNR salary issue, however, did have the desired effect, namely that of keeping regular hospital nurses in their positions. Nevertheless, hospitals were not going to pay their nurses at the same rate as those employed by the government's CNR without some form of compensation. Thus the Ministry of Health had little option but to fund part of the salaries of all hospital nurses. By doing so, it became the largest employer of nurses, and subsequently had a vested interest in nursing issues.

The implementation of the three-pronged approach had only narrowly succeeded in averting a total collapse of the nursing services. But averting a total collapse was not the same as providing an adequate nursing service across the country. There were still areas where hospital nursing services were non-existent or grossly inadequate. This situation could only be rectified by increasing the numbers of trained nurses. According to the GNC, there were over 80,000 registered nurses available for work; 24,000 were employed in the civilian sector and 9,000 in the military sector. It was estimated, therefore, that over 40,000 registered nurses had opted out of the profession. The government hoped to persuade these nurses to return to their profession, at least for the duration of the war.

With this aim in mind, the Ministry of Health spent over £166,000 on recruitment propaganda, which included a film entitled *The Lamp Still Burns* and starring some high profile film stars. Conscious of the fact that nursing possessed a proud military history, the film emphasised the connections between civilian and military nursing history, the heroic and vocational calling of nurses, and nursing as a valuable contribution to the overall war effort. The new nurse recruit is warned of the difficulties she will encounter on her road to registration, as this extract from the script reveals: "It's rather like joining the army, only a hospital is always at war against disease and accident. It's like training to be a commando. There simply isn't room for anyone who can't take it. And when you're in uniform my girl, everyone expects everything of you. And in order to give them what they expect, like any soldier, you have to be ready for any sacrifice."

But the script, which was written with the cooperation and assistance of the chief nursing officers at Whitehall, also emphasised the stupidity of petty rules and regulations. The message to hospital matrons was loud and clear. If they wanted more nurses then they would have to relax their attitudes towards nurse discipline, especially those rules that governed a nurse's private life.

For example, when the heroine of the propaganda film, having fallen foul of the matron over some petty misdemeanour, launches a verbal and emotional attack on the whole system of nurse training, the criticism of hospital matrons is only thinly disguised. As she is brought before the matron, the heroine argues that:

I am prepared to give up my personal freedom and live penned in by petty restrictions. I am even prepared to denounce my rights as a woman to a home and children of my own, because the demands of this profession leave no time for any personal life. I am prepared to submit to all this because I count it as a privilege to be allowed to devote my life to nursing. That's why I am grateful to you for giving me the opportunity to state my case, and why I beg you to let me stay on here no matter what the conditions. But are those conditions inevitable? They are not merely the result of wartime measures because it has always been like this, and there has always been a shortage of nurses. I don't believe they're inevitable and, because I care so much I urge you to agitate for their improvement. I implore you: start a reform, a complete reform. Because if you do, hospitals need never be understaffed again.

The message of the film fell on deaf ears, and matrons continued to claim that strict discipline was both necessary and character forming. They also argued that, on marrying, nurses needed to resign from the profession because the nature of the work made it impossible for a woman to combine the roles of wife and nurse. Some matrons, nonetheless, were prepared to make an exception for the duration of the war.

47

However, the reluctance of matrons to employ married women and relax disciplinary attitudes were not the only obstacles to nurse recruitment. Poor pay and long hours acted as a considerable deterrent, and the money invested in recruitment propaganda could not bear fruit unless these fundamental issues were confronted. In desperation the government appointed a committee to investigate nursing problems. The committee, chaired by Lord Rushcliffe, hastily introduced compulsory national pay scales for nurses and increased the salary divergence between trained and untrained staff. The implementation of the Rushcliffe proposals involved an additional expenditure of £2,750,000 and half of this cost was borne by the Exchequer. In addition to the salary improvements, a 96-hour fortnight was recommended for all nurses. Furthermore, in order to improve nurse distribution, the Control of Engagement Order, which had applied to other women between the ages of eighteen and forty, was now extended to include nurses.

Not for the first time the government succeeded in shooting itself in the foot. The Rushcliffe pay awards actually increased the nursing shortages, and in the very areas that were already suffering from a deficiency of nurses. Before the introduction of Rushcliffe scales, mental hospitals and sanatoriums were able to offer higher salaries to nurses; suddenly, they were no longer able to offer this incentive. Without the inducement of higher salaries, nurses abandoned these isolated and unpopular fields of nursing in favour of general nursing, although the midwifery sector benefited from a clause in the Control of Engagement Order that relinquished nurses from control if they embarked on further training courses. Most newly qualified staff did not want to be subjected to Ministry of Labour control so they opted instead to train as midwives. Overall, however, the implementation of the Rushcliffe pay awards and the extension of the Control of Engagement Order only succeeded in compounding an already severe situation. Even though Rushcliffe had recommended substantial salary increases for registered nurses, these increases failed to have any impact on the nursing situation. Salary improvements were negated by the fact that, between 1940 and 1943, the cost of living had risen by over 40 per cent.

Registered nurses were also dismayed by a GNC decision to extend the period of registered nurse training to that of four years instead of three. The GNC argued that a longer training period would improve nurse status and in turn improve recruitment. But the decision was entirely motivated by economic considerations. Now that Rushcliffe had increased the pay differentials between trained and untrained nurses, the Ministry of Health and individual hospitals wanted to keep nurse recruits in training as far as possible. Morale in the nursing profession sank to an all-time low. Then, just as registered nurses believed there could be no further attacks on their professional status, the government introduced the 1943 Nurses Act. This Act not only legitimised the position of the assistant nurse, but also allowed Christian Science nurses to adopt the title "nurse" without receiving any formal training whatsoever.

There was an outcry in the profession. One nurse remembered, "You would have thought that the world had caved in the way everyone went on!" But it was not surprising that registered nurses took such exception to the Act. Their status was not merely recognition for a lengthy period of training, it was also designed to protect the patient from charlatans. As the nursing press proclaimed, "It is almost incredible that, after the profession of nursing has existed in England for a quarter of a century, totally ignorant Ministers of the Crown should be permitted to smash up not only the status of an honourable profession but deprive the public of necessary safeguards to health and life." Senior nurses at the GNC and the College of Nursing adopted a pragmatic approach and sanctioned the Act. For many registered nurses, however, the legislation represented an outright betrayal of their professional ideals.

As registered nurses grappled with the constant attacks on their status, young recruits to the profession were becoming less willing to endure the outdated methods of training and discipline. Registered nurses had tried to enhance their status by professional means but the demands of war had undermined the whole profession. Even girls of fifteen were expected to suture wounds, feed premature babies, and attend post mortems; if they could do all this, how could registered nurses justify their own training? The shortage of nurses had meant that jobs were performed on the basis of who was available, not on what skills they possessed. In an attempt to improve its status, the profession clung desperately to its heroic military past and, if anything, became more, not less rigid about discipline and hospital traditions. Moreover, the regimentation in nursing practice was just as severe as it was before the war. As Margaret Broadley remembered, "Sisters came on duty to an immaculate ward, every patient's nose in line with the centre crease of the top sheet." Recruits who were unable or unwilling to submit to such discipline complained bitterly to the Ministry of Health:

The reign of the Sergeant Major still continues in very many wards and only results in the frequent resignation of trained and untrained staff. I greatly objected to the lack of privacy in the nurses' homes. Cupboards and drawers were periodically inspected by the home's sister; letters were given out irregularly through a hatch because it was said that nurses could not be trusted to take their own.

So many sisters set themselves up as demi-gods demanding blind obedience from their subordinates. The matron is often a person with a very primly starched cap and apron, who makes a daily inspection tour of the ward, while nurses stand with bated breath hoping she will not notice that the corner of number 26's bed is not quite straight.

Surely after the long hours we work we are entitled to a little recreation in our private lives. Most of the rules are petty, such as no flowers allowed in bedrooms, no shoes on the floor, nothing on the window sills or dressing tables, nurses to be indoors by 10.30p.m., lights out at 11p.m. No-one to take a bath after 10p.m. A round is done by the Home Sister to see that these rules are carried out.

The hardest task of all — is that of complying with all the petty restrictions, which in most cases are worse than the Armed Forces.

Priority is given to the tidying of lockers and straightening of beds before the care of patients.

Discipline developed into class distinction and obliteration of all feelings.

Within my own experience I found that there is a general feeling of suppression, one feels like a mouse must feel when tormented by a cat and cannot get free.

The senior staff needed to treat the junior staff as human beings and not as automatons. I have been in the Army as you see and though there is plenty of discipline and red tape there, there is still a more human element in it than I found in hospital.

Discipline was carried out to an extreme, so much so that it was frightening and disturbing.

Life on the wards was one long nightmare. I did my best with work that was entirely new to me, only to be severely reprimanded if anything was wrong, and usually in front of the patients. Sister never tried to help us, she was just there trying to find fault.

These extracts, taken from letters written by nurse recruits who had abandoned their training, provided the Ministry of Health with clear evidence of the main recruitment deterrent, but there was little or nothing that it could do to change matters. The military-style discipline was institutionalised in civilian nurse training, and had, in Victorian times, been accepted by most girls as onerous but necessary. The problem for the civilian nursing profession centred on a refusal to change with the times. With the outbreak of war, many women had gained a new independence and had embarked on a wide variety of careers. They were no longer satisfied with jobs like nursing, which demanded an increasingly unusual degree of subservience. As Monica Baly recalled, "There is no doubt about it, the discipline exerted in the schools of nursing was too strict. At St Thomas's, for example, they were being told to polish their brasses to the glory of God in 1938. But in 1941 they were no way going to polish their brasses to the glory of God."

Since the Ministry of Health could not persuade hospitals to relax their disciplinary codes and encourage more girls into nursing they decided to tackle the problem from another angle. Following long and drawn-out discussions with the Ministry of Labour and the War Office, the Ministry of Health decided to restrict the flow of nurses into the armed forces. Hospital matrons, assistant matrons, sister tutors, practising midwives, health visitors, practising district nurses, sanatorium nurses, sick children's nurses and mental nurses were all prevented from joining the military. In cases of severe nursing shortages, hospitals were also permitted to request the postponement of "call-up" with regard to nurses not in the aforementioned categories. Understandably, the War Office was very reluctant to agree to this restriction since it meant that only newly qualified nurses could now enter the forces. The armed forces needed experienced nurses, those who could cope under pressure, organise and supervise medical orderlies, and take the initiative in difficult situations. Up until this point, they had been able to recruit plenty of nurses of just the right calibre, but from 1943 onwards it was the turn of the military sector to bear the brunt of nursing shortages.

But the nursing situation in the civilian sector did not improve, despite the "carrot and stick" approach adopted by the government. There were, however, alternative strategies that would have yielded more nurses. There was a plentiful supply of women over the age of thirty-five who were rejected as recruits, having been told by hospital matrons that they were too old to nurse. Matrons preferred to employ young girls as they were considered to be more compliant than older women. Furthermore, although the marriage bar was lifted, many hospitals still insisted that nurses "lived in". Since married women were not likely to want to live apart from their husbands, the obligatory "live in" rule still precluded the employment of married nurses.

If the Ministry of Health had stepped in and made it compulsory for matrons to accept recruits regardless of their age, and insisted that the "live in" rule was abandoned, then it is likely that nursing shortages would have been alleviated, to some extent at least. But without this mandatory action, and without the cooperation of matrons, the government had no choice but to deprive the armed forces of experienced nurses.

More significantly, these restrictions on nurse conscription were extremely ill-timed. The organisation of military medical services had already been hampered by VAD problems. Now, just as Britain was about to wage war on a "second front", they were to be depleted in number and deprived of experienced nurses! The early pressures of war had shifted government policy with regard to nurses. Officials had recognised earlier administrative mistakes and had sought nursing advice. But the situation had not really changed for the better for civilian nurses. They had hoped that the war would bring opportunities for professional advancement, but although they had expanded their spheres of influence in some medical areas, they were actually working harder for less recognition. Registered nurse status was being attacked from all directions and, in desperation, just as they had done in previous years, civilian nurses looked again to their military colleagues for inspiration.

CHAPTER
THREE

The Move to Khaki

Military nurses experienced the "calm before the storm" in much the same way as their civilian counterparts. They were also forced to confront similar status problems, although the degree to which these problems impinged on everyday nursing practice varied between the services. Much depended on the numbers of VADs the individual forces were expected to accommodate. The Royal Air Force (RAF) managed to avoid many of the status problems associated with VAD nurses by creating their own Women's Auxiliary Air Force (WAAF) nursing orderlies. The Air Ministry had argued that an establishment of WAAF auxiliary nursing orderlies was an absolute necessity since "it was not considered desirable to employ VADs in small sickquarters in the RAF as most of the RAF stations were sited in sparsely inhabited parts of the country where accommodation outside RAF and WAAF quarters is difficult or impossible to find".

The Royal Navy (RN) accommodated more VADs than the RAF but the vast majority of VADs were incorporated within the Army and, consequently, the antagonisms which arose between registered nurses and

VADs were more visible within that service. The QA nurses were intent on proving their value to the Army, and by doing so they hoped to gain the military respect that had so far eluded them. For many years they had struggled to find their place within the Army framework. Seemingly, their only reward was to be viewed as a somewhat bizarre establishment. This view was reflected in the military nicknames that concentrated on the initials QAIMNS. According to military personnel, these initials stood for "Queer And Impossible, Mostly Not Sane". Or "Queer Assortment of Individuals, Mostly Not Sexed". Thus members of the Queen Alexandra's Imperial Military Nursing Service were the focus of some male military amusement. Neither did VADs escape similar treatment; they were dubbed "Virgins Almost Desperate". Male officers could not fully understand why women would want to be members of the military in the first place, while military nurses strove to be taken seriously, and failed to understand why male officers viewed their presence only in terms of boosting morale.

As Nurse Anne Moat recalled of her posting to France early in the war, "The Colonel did tell us when we got out there that they had decided to have nursing sisters as far forward as they could, because they had proved in the 1914-1918 War that the morale was so much improved the moment they saw the nursing sisters." Commanding officers believed that nurses were of value primarily because they provided soldiers with a constant reminder of what they were fighting for, namely their own wives, mothers, sisters and daughters. Most nurses accepted that they had this effect on the fighting men, but they themselves wanted recognition for their nursing skills. After all, the primary aim of military nursing and medical care was to get the injured man back into the thick of fighting. Monica Baly explained, "You had a pressure to get people back to duty, particularly in the Air Force where you were dealing with people like pilots who were very valuable and precious. You had to get them back into the air as quickly as possible." Given this pressure, military nurses, not unreasonably, concluded that they were in fact an essential cog in the military wheel. Moreover, as an integral part of the war machine they began to demand respect. As mentioned in chapter one, Dame Katherine Jones was the champion of military registered nurses and had formulated her militarisation policy during her time in Cherbourg with the British Expeditionary Force. In order to gain commissioned officer status, she claimed that Army nurses needed to be viewed as professional non-combatant officers. Their duties were outlined by Dame Katherine as follows: "To carry out their professional duties with the technical skill and knowledge produced by an arduous training, and supervise the work of nursing personnel. Accept responsibility for the discipline and organisation of the wards, and train Royal Army Medical Corps personnel in nursing duties." Thus Army nurses were the only women in the Army who were responsible for the training and supervision of male soldiers.

However, although Dame Katherine had a clear agenda, her nurses working at ground level were not always aware of her policy. The aims and ambitions of some military nurses did not extend beyond the desire to administer care where it was most needed, and to be valued as professionals. Others were so absorbed in their work that they initially failed to notice the small and gradual changes in nursing practice and protocol. In addition to the drill and physical training sessions, there were lessons on how to salute. Nurses were encouraged to adopt an air of brusque efficiency and to address each other by surnames. On the wards, military influence dictated nursing practice to the extent that patients were often attended to according to their rank, regardless of the severity of their injuries. All of these changes were small but insidious. The decision to move nurses into the frontline, however, was momentous.

Nevertheless, for the first few months of the war military nurses were not required to do much in the way of frontline nursing.

We got out to Dieppe and they said there was nothing doing at the moment, but we had to report every day to headquarters and they said we had to go off to the front, so off we went. Then we just shunted backwards and forwards. We didn't seem able to get any orders. However, we got up to beyond Lilles and we saw the French Army going up. It was pathetic — they were so scruffy. Horse drawn wooden carriages.

Colonel Margaret Kneebone recalled that:

We had gone over to Dieppe around the middle of May. We arrived at 5 in the evening and suddenly there was an air-raid warning and bombs were dropping all around. I was taking a shower at the time. We had to take our tin hats with us everywhere and I came out in my vest and tin hat. However, they didn't hit us and I couldn't believe that they would.

It was crowded and it was the first time that I had seen battle exhaustion. It was a pathetic sight. Their faces were blue, and they were just too tired to move. However, we got to a station and someone said, "Do you want a cup of tea sister?" So we sat over there and they had these enormous crates of stores and the French people were looting like mad. However, we were pleased to have that rather than the Germans.

We got the order to take no more patients. So I went to my Red Cross store and I got an enormous quantity of supplies; mittens, socks, gloves and everything else. I gathered them up and thought the Germans shan't have these, and I went and gave them to all the orderlies and anybody else who wanted them. Then just about midday whilst I was in the quartermaster's store a company officer, a very smart territorial, came to the door, saluted me and said, "Madam, the order has come, immediate movement, get into the ambulances and get outside the door. You cannot go to the billets and get your things. As you have had your lunch and we haven't, go to your store cupboard and gather up all the tinned food you can and as quickly as you can . . ." But there were four of my sisters down at the billet having lunch. Not one of them said a word. I brought them up on laws, not to question why, yours but to do or die!

For days and nights, ships of all kinds plied to and fro across the Channel under the fierce onslaught of the enemy's bombers. As each ship came in, the army doctors at the port would shout out to the captain on the bridge to ask for the number of wounded, and in a few minutes the ambulances and stretchers would be alongside to bring them off and take them to the waiting hospital trains in the station. The organisation of the port was excellent. The ships were being unloaded at an astonishing speed and no sooner were they empty than they were disappearing through the harbour entrance back to France to fetch more men home.

The Dunkirk evacuation, which took place between 26 May and 4 June 1940, signalled a turning-point. Both Britain and France had been ill-prepared for war, and the Allied high command had relied on an outdated and weak strategy. The German Blitzkrieg policy relied on lightning strikes and mobile forces, while the Allied forces were prepared to fight the First World War all over again. It was not the lack of equipment and resources that resulted in an Allied defeat at this stage, but a lack of inspired leadership. The German offensive in France began on 10 May 1940. Ten days later France had fallen and the Germans consolidated their position such that Britain was forced to evacuate its troops. The Germans had invaded near Sedan and, once they were over the Meuse, defeat was perhaps inevitable. The most rigorous of counter-attacks was staged by the British at Arras, and there were suggestions that this only failed because reserves were not forthcoming. But the problem was more fundamental. Blitzkrieg constituted a new and revolutionary form of warfare and, until the Allies had developed ways of beating it, they were doomed to failure.

There were, however, limits to the Blitzkrieg strategy. No amount of German Panzer divisions could reach Britain, because to do so would involve crossing the sea. Hitler could only envisage an invasion of Britain once the Royal Navy and the RAF had been subdued. The subsequent air battle between the RAF and the German Luftwaffe, which became known as the Battle of Britain, began on 10 July 1940 and proved to be crucial.

Monica Baly had a ringside seat of one aerial conflict that took place on 15 September 1940:

It was a golden September day, the sea was blue and calm and I was home on leave from hospital in Bexhill, having obtained the permit which confirmed that Bexhill was my home in what was now a defence zone. Our house was almost on the sea front, which was protected by barbed wire and concrete blocks, and mother was an ARP warden. Always on the look-out for a supplement to our diet, mother and I decided to take a picnic to Fairlight

Glen above Hastings and look for blackberries. We climbed up the deserted path and sat down and surveyed the absolute serenity of the English Channel, never had it looked more beautiful. Then, in the distance we heard the sound of aircraft — ours or theirs? Suddenly the sky was full of activity, we sat transfixed, waves of planes came over, sometimes we could see the markings and there unfolded before our eyes perhaps the greatest battle of the Second World War. There above us were Spitfires and Hurricanes intercepting with bursting gunfire, then one would see a plane on fire spiralling down to the sea. Was this it? Was this the dreaded invasion?

We reckoned we were as safe on the cliff as anywhere but thought that we ought to get home as soon as possible as best we could, so, forgetting the blackberries, we clambered down the path only to find Hastings in confusion. No one was sure what was happening except that there was a great battle going on overhead. Now our one thought was to get home to the wireless where the voice of Charles Gardiner in a legendary commentary gave an eyewitness account of what had happened and what was happening. Curiously, though one was chilled by the tragedy of burning aircraft which we had seen with our very eyes there was a sense of intense excitement. Later Gardiner was criticised for being carried away with emotion and making the whole thing sound like a football match, but that is how it seemed at the time. The reckoning and the burns I was soon to nurse in the Air Force came later. What we had witnessed was the pride of the Luftwaffe being picked off by some 300 Spitfires and Hurricanes.

By the end of September the Luftwaffe had lost 1,408 aircraft compared with Britain's loss of 697 aircraft. During this battle for air supremacy, over 500 British civilian hospitals were hit, and many civilians were killed. The conflict also severely affected air crews. The rapid speed with which aeroplanes on fire hurtled to the ground produced what became known as "Airman's Burns". These burns caused deep penetration and destruction of body tissues and were treated by sulphonamide powder and vaseline gauze. Eventually, less painful methods of treating burns were invented, such as the irrigation bag. Affected limbs were floated in a saline-filled bag, which provided continuous antiseptic and painless treatment. In addition to their physical injuries, pilots and air crew were also prone to psychological stress. This problem was not always immediately obvious to medical personnel but, nevertheless, became increasingly recognised as a possible consequence of battle. Monica Baly recalled how, "We were investigating the stress on air crews. We had learnt by the mistakes of the First World War, of which there were many — tragic of course. But these investigations revolutionised mental nursing. There was a changed attitude towards anxiety states, and one realised that they could be rehabilitated by the use of counselling, psychotherapy and so forth."

Research in the stress levels of air crews found that the pilot experienced lower levels of stress than the gunners. Psychologists concluded that this was because the pilot was forced to concentrate on the aeroplane's instruments and his mind was thus always occupied and focused, whereas the gunner believed himself to be a "sitting duck", as well as having too much time to dwell on the possible outcome of battle. As nurses working with the RAF soon discovered, when pilots crashed their aircraft, the crew were either killed instantly, suffered severe burns, or were found sitting by the wreckage of their planes having a cigarette. It was not surprising, therefore, that aircraft gunners visualised a "worst case" scenario.

The Battle of Britain was unique in that it was the first battle to be decided by air power alone. Hitler had expected that the air battle would clear the way for a land invasion. But the German defeat forced him to abandon Operation "Sealion", the code name for the proposed invasion of Britain. Instead, he chose to switch his attention to sea warfare and attempt to defeat Britain by means of a submarine blockade. Thus began the Battle for the Atlantic, a battle that turned out to be the longest campaign of the war.

Following the fall of France, the focus of public attention had shifted to the Mediterranean and North Africa. On 10 June 1940 Mussolini had entered the fray on the side of Hitler. The Italian population were not altogether convinced of the wisdom of this move but were, at this stage, powerless to prevent it. The Director of the British Medical Services reorganised the field ambulances in East Africa in expectation of heavy casualties, as revealed by War Office records:

> When Italy declared war one of her first warlike acts against East Africa was to bomb and machine-gun the aerodrome at Wajir. Lying at Habbaswein was the first heavy section of the Tanganyika Company of what was now the First Field Ambulance, with its light section just outside Wajir. This First Field Ambulance was composed of three companies, viz. Tanganyika, Kenya and Uganda Companies. Such an arrangement proved unwieldy, as companies were so big. Accordingly it was soon broken up, and each company, with a little expansion, made into a full field ambulance retaining, however, its old attributes of mobility and divisibility along with the capacity for major surgery and ability to "hold" patients indefinitely if required.

In October of the same year Italy invaded Greece and Britain supplied troops to support the Greek defence. The experiences of Fani Mavroudi-Theodoropoulou, a Greek nurse, are recounted in a report published in New York:

> I served at the Hospital of Loutraki from November 20th 1940 to April 1941 when the Germans invaded. Most of the wounded pleaded with the doctors to shorten their treatment so that they could return to the front. They asked us not to record a high

temperature on their charts so as to mislead the doctors. The attitude to our English allies was moving, as was the attitude towards the young German paratroopers (800 boys between the ages of 17 and 19) who had been brought to the Pallas hospital, all sustaining wounds after the battle at the Corinth Canal. They (the Greek soldiers) treated the young Germans with kindness and compassion and to the English, they tried at all times to express their gratitude. There were many examples of chivalry and hospitality. I remember a second lieutenant who had lost both his legs below the knees and dragged himself (they had not yet given him wooden legs) to the wards of the English to offer them cigarettes, candies and to tell us, the nurses, "Take care of them. Reduce our mess and give it to them because they are used to butter and marmalade, while we are used to sparse meals."

The same report describes the bravery of the Greek nurses:

While Greek soldiers throw themselves into battle with their arms and bayonets in order to keep Greece free from invasion, the nurses carry out a task which is equal in bravery and self denial to that of the army. Undaunted by weather conditions they continue the task of providing every possible treatment to the injured and the sick. The hospitals consist of tents in the snow, usually within earshot of the gunfire. These makeshift hospitals follow the army everywhere. The tents are folded and transported by lorry, many of them even by mule while the army is on the move. Whenever a move is necessary, the operating instruments, the storage heating, the mobile stoves, the folding beds, chairs and tables are loaded instantly. The nurses then take their own belongings. Normally, whenever they have to cross rivers whose bridges have been destroyed, the hospital articles are transported to the opposite shore by ropes and wheels, while the doctors and nurses cross the river on horseback or foot.

Churchill made much of Britain's support of Greece as he viewed them as an important ally. As the *War Illustrated* reported in November 1940:

History may have to record that the invasion of Greece was the beginning of the end of Mussolini's dominion. Certainly we have secured an ally of whom we may well be proud. "There is one small heroic country," declared Mr Winston Churchill in the peroration of his speech at the Lord Mayor's luncheon at the Mansion House on November the 9th, "to whom our thoughts today go out in new sympathy and admiration. To the valiant Greek people and their armies, now defending their native soil from the latest Italian outrage — to them we send from the heart of old London our faithful promise that amid all our burdens and anxieties we will do our best to aid them in their struggle, and we will never cease to strike at the foul aggressor in ever-increasing strength from this time forth until the crimes and treacheries which hang around the neck of Mussolini and disgrace the Italian name have been brought to condign and exemplary justice."

These were fine words, but in addition to offering support to the Greeks the British forces were also beginning a long struggle for the control of North Africa and the Middle East. As the troops prepared for battle, the nurses prepared for the wounded. One described the conditions:

We went into battle straightaway because they were waiting for us to put up this lines of communication hospital, because they were bringing casualties from the camp reception stations and we were the first port of call. They all arrived in the middle of the night around 12 o'clock, and then at 5 o'clock in the morning they started up the theatres and just went on the whole time. The nursing personnel went on the whole time for the whole day and the next day, and then they had half a day and started the same procedures again.

Dame Monica Goulding was matron during the campaign and remembered that:

the largest [reception of casualties] was when they were coming down from the western desert, when we used to have 300 casualties at a time. They were received in one of the large dining halls. We took over an Italian school and a barracks at Hillmere and they were all put on the floor as they were brought in, with their field medical cards which gave their disability, illness or whatever. It was so well organized, with the commanding officer, two of his seniors, always the consultant surgeon or the physician, and of course the quartermaster's staff; I always had either one of my assistant matrons and a divisional sister, and our job was to go up and down the lines and quickly sort out the ones which needed to be hurriedly got to the wards.

The classic example: I was going along looking at these cards and I heard a voice say, "Who's that? Is that you nurse?" and I went over and said, "Yes laddie, what is it?" I looked at his field medical card pinned on his battledress. Both hands were blown off. I thought it was dreadful. However, he said to me, "Who are you?" and I said, "I am matron." "Oh," he said, "you are just the one I want. Can I go into the ward with my friend because we have always been together and he'll help me, and I'll help him. He has lost his eyes." So I went to the commanding officer and I said, "Can they go to the same ward?" "Of course, my dear lady," he said, because normally he would have gone to the eye ward. They were wonderful! They both survived and went down to South Africa to convalesce, but they were eyes and hands to each other. I shall never forget those two.

There were also times when nurses experienced real fear, not only for their own safety, but for the patients under their care. As Monica Baly recalled:

I do remember there, on night duty, going around the huts with just my little hurricane lamp, and being quite frightened, particularly where patients were very ill because I couldn't note the change in their condition and that sort of thing. And of course, walking across, right on the edge of the desert, with the jackals calling, it really was quite a frightening experience.

They had been arguing about the extended role of the nurse since Nightingale was a girl, but if you're pressed to it you will get on and do it. I remember recently when there was all this hoohar about a girl who was allowed to finish sewing up for an appendix operation, and the story hit the news headlines. Well, those of us who had been in the armed services said, "So what?" A friend of mine who had been a very good theatre sister out in the Middle East said, "What do they suppose we did in the desert?"

Desert warfare brought significant health problems, most of which were caused by the intense heat and a lack of water. As Colonel Ursula Dowling explained:

At the time we were in grey cotton dresses and we looked like little orphan Annies. The water was brought in overground by pipe. The water was always brown so we had to give up wearing caps because they were brown and white overalls turned brown, you see. You couldn't wash them because the water was brown and we had no stockings by that time of course. I had lost all my shoes — they had been lost out of my bed-roll and I was wearing men's shoes which I had got from the officers' shop. But they were a bit big and clumsy.

There were also instances of nurses being forced, through circumstances, to wear men's uniforms, much to the amusement of their male colleagues.

But despite the many problems associated with administering medical care in the desert, in some cases the conditions actually assisted the healing process.

The worst things I remember of Egypt were the flies and dust. The flies were frightful. As you were dressing the patients they would come around in swarms, but of course they had been using the Trueta treatment of cleaning them up on the battlefield, and although when you got them back and came to dress them they were often crawling with maggots and the patients used to think it was dreadful, you got used to it. You would say to them, "Don't worry, tomorrow it will be alright", and of course it was just nature's way of healing. Those wounds healed beautifully.

The Trueta treatment of cleaning wounds on the battlefield was again the result of information gained during the Spanish Civil War. Professor Trueta was a

Spanish surgeon who had worked as the chief of a large surgical unit in Barcelona. Trueta had discovered that, unless injuries received immediate "on the spot" skilled attention, subsequent treatment was very often useless. This discovery had not been acknowledged by the British civilian medical services during the planning of the emergency services, but it had been taken on board by the military. Whereas in previous wars field ambulances had always followed the brigades, from 1939 onwards the field ambulances were situated at the front. More vehicles were lost by adopting this strategy, but more lives were saved. The need to maintain troop mobility, however, was paramount. Medical units were smaller and more mobile than they had been in previous conflicts because the nature of warfare itself had changed. Troops needed to cover large geographical areas and be able to move at a moment's notice. Swift enemy advances highlighted the importance of mobility. Desert warfare was conducted on much the same lines as sea warfare, with motorised tank divisions fighting "on the move" rather than adopting static positions.

Dressing stations needed to be far enough forward to provide attention to the wounded, but not too far forward lest they impede the fighting forces. They also needed to be instantly recognisable and easy to locate. Equipment was packed in such a way that medical personnel knew exactly where to find everything. Practical considerations had also rendered the traditional QA uniform obsolete. As the militarising Matron-in-Chief explained:

It is clearly impossible, for a service of over 10,000 women, many of them overseas, to continue to wear a uniform which, though beautiful in itself and rich in honourable tradition, is not suitable for conditions in active service in camps and deserts, jungles and shipwrecks, or even at home under stress of clothing rationing and cleaning difficulties. These circumstances, as well as the danger of machine-gun bullets and the ruining of camouflage, have driven us into outdoor khaki uniform and even into battledress, slacks and ATS AA boots and anklets. I think that Florence Nightingale, if she were alive now, would rejoice in the significance of this unfeminine apparel, for it means that we are getting ever closer to the frontline.

In addition to the change in uniform, there were also changes in discipline. The demands of war had led to a more relaxed working environment in some instances. Medical personnel worked as a team and paid little attention to military hierarchy. Nurses also found that they were able to use their initiative and adapt to rapidly changing circumstances, as Monica Baly agreed:

Whether at home or abroad, shortage of supplies and difficult working conditions meant that you had to make do and improvise. Nurses found themselves very good at improvising, and also discovered that a lot of things that had been done by rote for years, and that they had been trained to do, were actually no longer necessary. You found, in fact, that when the bombs were falling you could get patients out of bed immediately after an operation and they didn't die. You could operate on patients without them being starved for 24 hours and it didn't matter very much. It was cook book nursing to some extent and we followed the recipe. We found, as well, that we could make other recipes for ourselves.

These made-up "recipes" included new medical advances like blood transfusions:

We had refrigerated vans, the troops used to call them the "vampire vans". The blood supplies were kept up all the time. We must have taken some over with us and I know there was a system of vans going round all the units. It was a sort of centrifugal refrigerator, if I remember rightly, so that the blood was stirring all the time. I'm not terribly sure how it was preserved. But I know that there were refrigerated vans which carried out this service and we were never short.

Blood supplies were usually maintained, but confused or interrupted orders often made deliveries, of other medical supplies as well as blood, difficult. At times, nursing sisters had no idea of their destination and, even when they were told, strict censorship rules operated. They were not allowed to divulge their whereabouts to relatives and friends, and not permitted to write about the treatment of their casualties. The following letter,

75

written on 1 May 1941 by a military nurse to the matron of the Royal London Hospital, demonstrates the rigidity of the censorship rules:

Dear Matron,

I had intended writing a letter to include a description of our work here, but just now the CO sent a chit round to all of us to say that no details of this must be put into letters, so I will try and make my letter interesting and at the same time comply with the censor's rules. When we left we had no idea where our port of embarkation was, but soon found out where we were heading, and personally I did have a few qualms as the train galloped through my beloved country. We arrived at our destination in a thick fog and I left most of my bags behind as we stumbled and fell about the docks, until we found our boat. It was amazing how very quickly we all settled down. We were part of the [— censored word omitted] up till then [— censored word omitted] largest convoys to leave Britain, and each boat was, to say the least of it, very full. I shared a cabin with P. O'Sullivan and another sister, and I must say they made very pleasant stable companions. We had to make ourselves a strict routine for dressing, etc., as the cabin in peacetime would certainly have not held three! Never in our lives shall those who stayed up to see the last of Britain forget the night we left. In the morning the fog lifted and we slowly, but surely, went up the river, staying when we got to the mouth for the convoy to collect. A rumour went round, as they will, that we were to move out at midnight — and we did. A brilliantly moonlit night and the bay full of boats, some waiting to go down the river, us to go out, and lots just waiting. They all had tiny lights forward and aft, and those about to move had pilot lights as well. From shore, both sides of the river, beacons flashed signals, and from the naval boats and from us, as the commodore boat, answering signals.

Then quite quietly the naval escort moved out. I can't give you numbers or names, but believe me it was a flattering number, and made you feel really safe. They looked marvellous silhouetted against the shining water. After they had slipped through the boom, we followed, with siren shrieking, and all the boats in the harbour gave answering hoots of farewell. It was most impressive. By morning we were well away and had joined the rest of the convoy, coming, I suppose, from different ports. It was nothing like I had expected a convoy to be — either in size or in the way it was managed. We had a good deal to thank both the Navy and our own ship's staff. Life in the boat could have been very boring had we not determined it should not be. We had 38 sisters on our particular ship, nearly eight to one in officers, and countless troops. We took it in turns, two on two days at a time, to be on duty in the hospital. We all enjoyed that. I represented the sisters on the Entertainments Committee, and worked jolly hard. We had also a terrifically enterprising Sports Committee and Library Committee. As far as entertainments were concerned, we were lucky in having six professional actors and a cartoonist on board. Our main object was to entertain the troops, but I must confess the officers and sisters were always anxious to be entertained too! We got up a series of concerts, serious music, bridge, chess and whist drives. Everything you prepared had to be performed at least seven times to ensure that all the men had a chance of seeing it, so that we always had 60-70 people working hard. We also had a "Crossing the Line" ceremony and a circus. The troops loved these. The sports people of course, dealt with boxing, PT, deck games, etc. Every morning we had three lectures each lasting three quarters of an hour. This we found was a very wise movement on the part of OC troops — it kept you all away from each other. Lectures in Hindustani, medicine, and then one of general interest, such as travel, books, etc. These were of course the nicest. The last night on board we had community singing on deck; the whole ship took part and it really was a marvellous effort. The many weeks on board, because of our activities, flew.

The entertainment and activity on board the troopships were designed to relieve some of the tension that frequently arose when troops were crammed together for long periods. Entertainment also boosted morale and provided a welcome distraction. But as the war progressed, such distractions became more of a luxury. One QA nurse described her experiences as follows:

We were in a convoy of 75 ships; this was not the largest convoy, but I was told it was an important one, apart from the number of troops carried. There was a great number of cargo boats and some of the troopers looked as if they would never reach any destination, by their derelict appearance. They all did, however, with the exception of two. A Commodore was in charge of the convoy, the Vice Commodore was on our ship. A few days after we were at sea, orders came through that our draft was cancelled. Nevertheless, we continued on our way over the ocean as the convoy could not stop to take us off or return us to England. We had several alarms from unidentified planes, but no action took place. We had 7,000 troops on board our ship and 700 officers, including we sisters and VADs. There were a few Army sisters, and Army medical officers who were in charge of a mobile theatre unit destined for Egypt. Life on board ship was very spartan, and exceeded any tales we had ever heard about life on a troopship. The worst part was the lack of air-conditioning, as our ship was a North Atlantic Passenger Liner in peacetime, and had no amenities for the tropics. There were no chairs, so we all sat out on the deck, using our rugs spread out and our lifejackets as a cushion, when we could all find enough space to spread ourselves out to this extent.

Boat drill was a serious daily routine, a few women being allocated to each life-boat.

The ship was in the charge of the RAF. A band was quickly improvised by Con Dockerty, who used to play the organ at the Gaumont Cinema, Hammersmith. Occasionally, they gave concerts in the lounge, or played in the saloon, when one of the senior officers had a birthday, or any other cause for celebration. The men had concerts most evenings. No wireless, gramophone or singing on deck was permissible, in case of attracting the attention of U-boats.

No ceremony was allowed when "crossing the line", neither would the captain allow any awning up (in case of attack from the air), so we suffered very much from the tropical sun. Those who had not bought a topee were issued with Army ones (what an indignity for a naval sister!) and very funny some of them looked too! One sister, being about 5 ft high, looked just like a mushroom!

As the letter suggests, naval nurses were most indignant at having to wear any part of Army issue uniforms. With regard to the planning of individual campaigns and the provision of medical backup, all three services worked together, but there was plenty of friendly rivalry. Each service claimed to be the most efficient, most enthusiastic, and the most well presented, and it was thus considered quite humiliating to be forced by circumstances to wear the uniform of another service. Inter-service rivalry was encouraged by the high-ranking officers as a means of keeping the members of the forces "on their toes", and competition became even more intense when these members were subjected to examinations. Results were open to scrutiny, and the personnel in one service invariably measured their results against colleagues in another. However, during the lecture programmes and examinations that were conducted on board troopships, and in other situations where service men and women were confined for long periods, a different rivalry emerged.

Much to the horror of male military officers, many of the women were obtaining higher examination marks than the men. In some cases, the nursing sisters were even outstripping the male officers! This caused a considerable amount of consternation, and some officers accused individual examiners of favouritism or of "making allowances" for the sisters because they were women. Examination subjects usually covered a wide curriculum and encompassed new medical procedures, general safety in a variety of war zones, and obscure languages such as Hindustani. Nursing sisters studied intensely and their efforts were rewarded. Despite the "sour grapes" that were displayed by some military officers, nursing sisters had proved that they could compete on the same terms as their male colleagues. The long-standing tradition of inter-service rivalry was, thereafter, partially superseded by the battle of the sexes!

But while the forces came to terms with the battle of the sexes, the more important battle against Hitler continued. The British troops were still playing a "cat and mouse" game with the Germans and Italians across the deserts of North Africa and the Middle East. In September 1940 Marshal Graziani and the Italian Tenth Army, supported by the Italian Air Force, had marched into Egypt. The Italians proceeded to establish a series of military camps covering a land mass of about 40 miles inland from Sidi Barrani. They also formed some camps at the rear. Their aim was to fortify positions and begin an offensive once their severely depleted supplies had been replenished. In the meantime, the British tormented the Italians by conducting a series of raids designed to disrupt communication networks. By November 1940 the Italians had still not resumed any offensive manoeuvres and the British, under the leadership of Sir Richard O'Connor, began to assume control. Italian forces far outnumbered the British, but O'Connor, who was in charge of the 7th Armoured Division and the 4th Indian Division, laid great emphasis on the importance of mounting a surprise attack. Thus British troops advanced under the cover of darkness, and on 7 December initiated an impressive offensive.

During the first 24 hours of the offensive, O'Connor's troops had demolished three Italian camps, and after 72 hours the British had taken over 40,000 prisoners. Buoyed with success, O'Connor moved forward towards Bardia and Tobruk, though the 4th Indian Division was replaced by the 6th Australian Division. The battle for Bardia was virtually won when the Australians entered the fortress on 3 January 1941, though it took another two days for victory to be assured. Tobruk managed to hold out against the British for two weeks before capitulating. Thus in a period of just two months the

Italians had been ousted from their positions in Egypt and East Cyrenaica, and O'Connor turned his attention towards West Cyrenaica and Tripoli.

While the 6th Australian Division travelled along the coastline, the 7th Armoured Division confronted the desert wastes just south of Jebel Achdar. The Italians were able to form ad hoc pockets of resistance but no durable organised defence, and as the 7th Armoured Division reached the coast the Battle of Beda Fomm ensued. For the three days between 5 and 7 February 1941 the battle raged, until the Italians, who were tired and disorganised, surrendered. Clearly, this British campaign was a tremendous success. From the beginning of the British offensive strike in December 1940 to the success at Beda Fomm, the British troops had advanced a distance of 400 miles. They had also captured valuable supplies and equipment, and over 130,000 prisoners. Not surprisingly, a confident O'Connor was keen to press on towards Tripoli. However, Churchill's promise to support the Greek defence against the Italians interfered with this goal. The Western Desert Force was the only "combat prepared" force readily available to fulfil Churchill's promise. Therefore, instead of advancing to Tripoli, the 6th Australian Division was sent to Greece alongside a contingent of New Zealand troops, and the 7th Armoured Division was sent to Egypt for some respite. Cyrenaica, meanwhile, was guarded by new Australian troops and one armoured division.

This British move was also prudent since the Germans had sent forces to Tripoli in support of their Italian allies.

The new German unit under the leadership of Erwin Rommel became known as the Deutsches Afrika Korps. Rommel's orders were merely to defend Tripoli. However, because British troops were mainly concentrated in Greece and East Africa, he seized the opportunity for an offensive campaign. The fighting resumed, and by 9 April the Germans had captured the British troops at Cyrenaica. The British retreated towards Egypt and also prepared to defend the fortress position of Tobruk. With the sea behind them, they were able to rely on the Royal Navy to bring in troop reinforcements and supplies whenever necessary. The Navy also provided a reasonable evacuation system for the wounded troops. The field hospitals, meanwhile, were coping as best they could:

After five weeks, we opened the hospital with the minimum of equipment and the convoys of sick and wounded started to arrive by sea. We worked partly in buildings, partly in tents. It was now growing warmer so we had no great anxiety over heating arrangements, but the sanitary conditions gave much food for thought. The Red Cross were marvellous in supplying us with requisites for the men, most of whom came to us with no toilet accessories whatever. I remember once, when we received over 100 ship wreck survivors, they came to me with supplies before I even knew that the men were coming in!

Another nursing sister working in the Middle East described her experiences in Baghdad with the 24 combined General Hospital:

Baghdad has always given me the impression of being an island standing in the middle of the ocean, only the sea is of sand; you can travel for miles in any direction and see nothing but desert. Everyone has heard of the "thief of Baghdad". We discovered that he has hundreds of descendants! The Baghdad Iraqi, like most town Arabs, is out to "do" his own grandmother and, since we couldn't claim even this relationship, we didn't stand a chance! The prices in most of the shops were impossible and we did not find the "man in the street" too courteous. A trial "blackout" took place soon after our arrival, but it proved such a Godsend to the local gentry, who took the opportunity to murder and steal with great gusto, that it was thought that even a bomb might cause less damage!

The hospital was a tented one of, nominally, 600 beds (we sometimes had nearly double the number of patients) in 100 bedded sections spread well apart, one section British and five Indian. The tentage was painted reddish-brown, as camouflage. Alas! Later, when the "rains came" the camouflage "came off" and descended in drips from unexpected angles on to us and the patients, till we looked somewhat like clowns in a circus.

The hospital was already working, and at great pressure, when we arrived, owing to a tremendous influx of malaria. The matron of 35 general hospital (not then functioning), and two sisters loaned from other hospitals, were helping the men to stem the tide when we relieved them. Our own matron did not join us until a few weeks later. It was a new experience to me to work in a hospital with Indian patients and run almost entirely by Indians. The Indian, on the whole, makes an ideal patient, and is very grateful for anything that is done for him. The greatest difficulty was in overcoming the prejudice in allowing sisters to go on night-duty. "It is your sex; it is your sex!" I was told patiently over and over again, to which I replied (less patiently I fear as time went on) that, though I could not be held responsible for the unfortunate fact of our sex, I definitely was for the nursing of the patients and must insist on having a sister in charge of any ward, both day and night, where there were very ill men.

Nursing sisters were often faced with prejudice, and both Indian and African male staff displayed incredulous disbelief at the nature of the nursing work. In West Africa hospitals were established courtesy of the War Office and employed as many Africans as possible. The 200- and 600-bedded hospitals were housed in purpose-built mosquito-proofed buildings, and tents were used to expand facilities as the numbers of wounded increased. Often the nurses had no proper accommodation and were housed in tents or disused buildings. Some nurses had simply to wait until accommodation was ready before catching up with their hospital. The numbers of hospitals increased as the war progressed, but at no time could the building schedule keep pace with the number of casualties. There was also a shortage of air-ambulances and hospital ships. Because of the growing number of casualties, two hospital ships were forced to act as stationary hospitals in the harbour. Some problems were to be expected, others were the result of gross inefficiency. Air-ambulances ordered for West Africa took several months to arrive, and when they did, military personnel discovered that the doors were not wide enough for stretchers to pass through. Consequently, they were forced to depend on the RAF for the airlift of casualties. Moreover, since the hospitals in West Africa were overflowing with casualties, large numbers of wounded personnel were transported to South Africa. As officials at the War Office acknowledged:

South Africa were very good in not only taking Imperial troops, but they also accepted Free French, Poles, Greeks and other invalids. There was one sad episode with regard to South Africa. When it came to installing the hospital at Cape Town, South Africa couldn't provide all the medical officers and all the sisters. Because of political differences with regard to the status of the sisters the matron-in-chief chose a most excellent batch of some 30 sisters, good at their jobs and all very pretty girls. Unfortunately they were all lost on the way out, on SS *Seramic*.

The political problems that surrounded the issue of registered nurse status had obviously not subsided since it was clear that the issue was still dictating military nursing policy. The sisters who were killed on SS *Seramic* were all young, and eager to administer care where it was most needed. They were also victims of the military assimilation policy. The status problems that beleaguered the military nursing profession, however, were not unique. Women who worked as qualified doctors in civilian society were also experiencing problems within the military framework. As female medical officers they were obliged to work without commissions at the beginning of the war. Following a substantial amount of lobbying from the Women's Medical Federation, they were eventually allowed to hold commissioned officer rank within the ATS (May 1941) but could not hold that commission if they were serving with the RAMC. The War Office justified this action as follows:

> You will note that in para 7 they slur over the fact that commissions in the land forces would give women disciplinary power over soldiers which the giving of commissions to women was designed to avoid in the case of other ranks of ATS and male officers. It is not merely a question of "qualities of medicine and leadership". It is the power of discipline over men which is the crux of the problem. Their medical professional equality is fully recognised, either with a commission in the

Women's Forces or without one, serving as women medical officers with the Royal Army Medical Corps.

In the case of female medical officers, a compromise solution was reached whereby they obtained commissions in the women's services for service with the RAMC. The nursing situation was somewhat different. Military personnel had apparently overlooked the fact that nursing sisters had always had power over men. They had long been responsible for the training of male RAMC orderlies and, as a consequence, were responsible for exerting discipline. Since the War Office had not objected to this practice, why had they objected so strongly in the case of female doctors? The reasons are not totally clear, but there seemed to be a general acceptance that medicine was a male profession and should be protected as such. Medicine was viewed as efficient, clinical and scientific and, because medical schools had only just begun to open their doors to women, medicine was still a predominantly male domain.

In contrast, nursing was viewed as a female profession, and one which incorporated the supposedly natural female characteristics such as nurturing and caring. Furthermore, although the RAMC was composed of military men, many of these were conscientious objectors. There was a long-standing military belief that somehow the RAMC did not consist of "proper men", that is, those who would fight for their country. It was, therefore, perfectly acceptable for these men to take orders from women. It can also be argued that the military was eager to give its nursing units a high profile as "gentle, feminine ministering angels", always at hand to offer comfort to the wounded, in order to emphasise the overall masculinity of the forces. It was not surprising, then, that early on in the war the Matron-in-Chief had insisted that nurses adopted the image of masculine efficiency in preference to the ministering angel. The change of image from angel to battleaxe was just another step on the road to commissioned officer status and full military recognition of the worth of registered nurses. As Dame Katherine herself acknowledged: "If I survive at all in nursing history I shall doubtless survive as the militarising Matron-in-Chief. I am glad that it should be so."

In 1941 Dame Katherine attained her primary objective as full commissioned officer status was afforded to military registered nurses. This event was also significant for civilian registered nurses, since they now had a point of reference for their own status. As the militarising Matron-in-Chief explained to the civilian Association of Hospital Matrons:

> To me, officer rank with all its symbols, its privileges, its duties and its traditions, is a living reality. It means responsibility and hard-earned privilege reflecting professional and military achievement. Can you therefore be surprised that conferment of commissioned rank on the Queen Alexandra's Imperial Military Nursing Service and the Territorial Army Nursing Service was the most

significant day of my working life. To me it was recognition of the status which a State Registered Nurse should enjoy in relation to auxiliary personnel.

Dame Katherine further explained how this event affected civilian nurses:

It was inevitable therefore that the commissioning of the QAIMNS and the TANS — and I want you to understand this as the imposition of the military rank pattern on the nursing profession — seemed to me an event of the first importance. By superimposing this rank pattern of the Army on one particular section of the nursing profession, it seemed possible, not merely to confer a status but to provide a framework which would hold that status firmly in place.

The nursing press reported the news with glee, and waxed lyrical about the military nurses' khaki uniforms and their new commissioned officer status. However, in addition to providing full military recognition to professional nurses, the War Office also believed that officer status would offer nurses some protection against bad treatment in the event of capture. This belief was unfounded. But despite the risks involved, the frontline nursing policy continued.

CHAPTER
FOUR

An Officer and a Lady

Although the Matron-in-Chief had fought hard to gain commissioned officer status for her nurses, not all her nurses appreciated the prize. Some nurses, particularly those from the Commonwealth, viewed the commissions as an unwelcome military imposition on their profession. They believed that nursing was essentially a civilian vocation. In Nightingale's day the introduction of female nursing into the services had been a means of bringing a gentler, more feminine and civilian approach to the realms of military medical care. Now the reverse was happening. Female military nursing no longer represented the "gentle touch". Instead, nursing sisters were encouraged to call each other by surnames, exchange salutes with their fellow officers and administer care in a brisk, orderly fashion according to rank. The formality of these practices was particularly resented by Commonwealth nurses. They had decided that the British were obsessed with military etiquette. As Jan Bassett observed in her study of Australian nursing services, the differences between British and Australian nurses were deep-rooted. The two groups still had very different concepts of army nursing. Dulcie Thompson says of the QAs: "The British girls, they of course had a much longer regular Army tradition. They had a stricter attitude — more traditional military attitude. Some British doctors were difficult and expected too much attention to rank, etc. This also applied to British matrons and some sisters. I think they felt the Australians of all ranks were too informal and friendly."

The Australian girls were also more likely to see the funny side of the militarisation process. Australian sister Jean Crameri recalled that:

> We have a route march every morning — Matron (Nell Marshall) takes us — we are away for about an hour and have many laughs . . . The other day Matron thought we would have some practice at Eyes Right. So she placed a nurse as Governor and we all turned Eyes Right. Then instead of Eyes Front Matron sang out Eyes Left — everyone roared laughing. You would really have to see her to appreciate her taking us for drill — she is such a tiny little thing.

It was not surprising, however, that British nurses were more enamoured with their new status than their Commonwealth colleagues. The British nursing profession had suffered from a low status and an even lower morale for decades. The fact that the military had recognised the value of registered nurses and had afforded them commissioned officer status acted as an important boost for the whole profession. However, as Dame Katherine pointed out, the officer status needed to be rigorously emphasised at every opportunity:

It is possible to hold a rank in the eyes of the Army Council but not in the eyes of the general public. There was a danger — there is still a danger — of QAIMNS enjoying the shadow of their rank without experiencing its substance. I illustrate this by two instances:

A senior QAIMNS officer wearing the relative rank badges of a Lieut. Colonel on the traditional uniform of the QAIMNS stood waiting for a lift in the company of a junior ATS subaltern (Lieutenant). Seeing two persons waiting, the lift attendant turned to the Lieut. Colonel and said, "Please wait a minute 'nurse' while I take the 'lady officer' up."

The QAIMNS' Principal Matron did not mind the few minutes' delay and in fact she told the story with some amusement, but what she really minded, and what I mind, and ask you to mind on her behalf, is the attitude to the nursing profession, of which such a remark is proof.

Again, in certain units all officers and other ranks male and female, that is, Army, QAIMNS and ATS, have orders to salute one another within the unit. In small units there is one QAIMNS sister and what has happened? It transpired that, although she was a commissioned officer and wore her rank badges on indoor and outdoor uniform, she was not saluted. She was, of course, known to all the officers and other ranks as the sister, but she was looked upon as a "nurse" or some category not quite that of an officer to whom the courtesy of a military salute was due.

Such incidents show how far we still have to go if we are to secure for State Registered Nurses in the Army the true status of a professional worker with officer responsibilities. The conferment of a commission is not enough — with the commission must go the most complete assimilation to the Army pattern if it is to be generally understood both inside and outside the Army.

While the Matron-in-Chief carefully monitored the level of military acceptance of nurse officers, nurses were told to guard their officer privileges. But there were some more light-hearted moments with regard to their newly acquired positions:

You had to learn to salute and say "Mam" and life was quite different. In fact, there was one rather amusing incident in Canada. We were all given ranks — we were Lieutenants and our matron was a Major. So when they saw Major Dyson on the list she was put in with a whole load of men. There was a great furore and they had to change everyone round on the ship in order that she got a cabin to herself.

Of course, we had a terrific matron. She was with us all the time and she made us aware of our responsibilities. She called us together one evening and she said, "And when you are in the dining-room" — she always called it the dining-room although they were just washed trestle tables, sand and the marquee — "we do not discuss shop in the regular service." The other thing she told us was that we were always to maintain our sense of duty, and that at no time should we expose ourselves to the heat, because we were there to render service to the troops.

Clearly 1941 was an important year for military nurses as they adapted to their new officer roles. It was also an important year for wartime Britain. O'Connor's military successes in the North African desert had boosted British morale, particularly since they had followed the RAF victory in the Battle of Britain. Churchill stepped up the campaign in North Africa following the British withdrawal from Crete on 1 June. This decision was taken partly to make up for the loss of Greece, and partly to stage a stronger counter-offensive against mounting German forces. The battle for the control of the Mediterranean Sea was also intensified. Most of the supplies to British troops in North Africa were shipped across the Mediterranean. The outcome of the desert battles was, therefore, largely dependent on the outcome of sea warfare. Meanwhile, Hitler turned his attention to the east. Despite the non-aggression pact that he had earlier signed with Stalin, his supposed ally, in June 1941 the Germans invaded Russia. Later in the year, on 7 December, Japan attacked the American naval base at Pearl Harbor and America entered the war on the side of Britain. The long struggle of "going it alone" since the fall of France had ended, and the tide began to turn in Britain's favour.

Because of the changing nature of wartime relationships nurses were confronted with a new category of patients seeking medical care.

In the spring of 1942, the Russians began releasing thousands of Poles, men, women and children, across the Caspian Sea, into Persia. These unfortunates arrived in a pitiable condition, the majority showing signs of several years of life under bad conditions, many of ill treatment. Hundreds were stricken with typhus, many died on the road, others survived a bare few hours after admission to hospital. 34 combined General Hospital, the first hospital to arrive in this area (Persia), worked in tents on a small stretch of desert about four miles out of Teheran, in order to prevent the spread of infection. They bore the brunt of the typhus epidemic. A Matron and nine sisters, including myself, came up from Iraq to join 18 Indian General Hospital in May and were given a site immediately adjoining 34. The Matron and sisters of 34 combined General Hospital were more than kind to us on arrival. In spite of their already heavy work, they provided meals for us for the first two days till our own cook house was in a condition to function.

Needless to say, several of our sisters gave them assistance on their wards till our own hospital was in working order. All those in the typhus wards wore white pyjama-suits over their clothes, tied at the waist, wrists and ankles, their heads swathed in a white cloth to afford protection from lice. The number of these people who recovered under proper treatment was especially gratifying when one considered the state that many of them were in before the typhus attacked them.

The numbers admitted with typhus began falling off after our arrival and by the time we were ready to function we took the ordinary sick, of which there were many. As our patients increased, more sisters were sent to us. We admitted men and boys only, except for one section for Polish ATS. We were also in tents and every drop of water had to be brought by water-cart, so that we had to use it carefully.

We were truly a cosmopolitan outfit: British sisters nursing Poles, in a purely Indian Hospital, in the middle of Persia. The Medical Officers all spoke English of course, and we had the odd Anglo-Indian orderly; otherwise the language situation was truly comic. It is extraordinary, though, how quickly one can get used to grasping a "sense" of what people are trying to say. We had several Polish ATS working in the wards. Though completely untrained on arrival, most of them proved very good, and one or two of them understood a little French, which was a great help.

Nurse Johnston, a sister with the QAIMNS Reserve, wrote of the release of Polish prisoners of war:

There must have been thousands of these first arrivals. Practically every disease in medical knowledge could be found among them and particularly deficiency diseases, dysentery, typhus and malaria.

Great difficulty was at first experienced in ascertaining the patients' names and this sometimes led to difficult situations, as for example, when a Jewish patient suddenly disappeared and after three days search was discovered to have died and been duly buried in a Roman Catholic grave. The error was rectified to the satisfaction of everyone concerned including, I hope, the Jew. Eventually we found there was an RAMC orderly who spoke Russian, French and German, and he was made responsible for seeing every new patient and obtaining their name, religion, etc.

In addition to the language difficulty there was of course the caste system among the sepoys and Indian followers. The sweepers would sweep, deal with latrines and bedpans, soiled linen and water; the bhesties would deal with clean water and linen only; the ward boys would deal with food and feeding utensils only; the sepoys would make beds but not touch any soiled linen of dysentery patients, neither would they touch a bedpan or help any patient with one no matter how ill the man might be. They could not be relied upon to wash the hands and face of any patient and had an intense dislike of touching dead bodies. The medical officers were fully employed doing the round of patients. The

RAMC orderly and the sister were the only people available at any time for any job from pitching tents and removing the dead to giving intravenous injections or dressing wounds.

My first reaction was to collect materials and spend 1 hour cleaning the mouth of a man who was obviously near the end of his life but having much difficulty breathing his last. An hour later a sepoy came to tell me he was dead. That incident snapped something in me and it was suddenly clear what, in broad outline, must be done. The individual must be sacrificed; for one trained person to cope with 200 or so in this condition it was obviously impossible to nurse even a fraction as they should be nursed, until the place was properly organized. In each section the same conclusion was reached sooner or later.

The staffing of the section included:

Trained personnel———————— One medical officer
One sister

Trained during the war————— One Anglo-Indian
RAMC orderly

Untrained———————————— 8 or 10 Sepoys

Followers doing the
work of their caste————— 2 ward boys
2 bhesties
2 sweepers plus one
on night duty.

Language barriers were a common dilemma within medical teams in nearly all the theatres of war. There were also problems associated with controlling the patients. Nursing sisters were used to patients staying in their beds for the duration of their illness — or at the very least staying in their wards. The patients in Persia had other ideas, as described in the following letter:

The discipline among these people was not such as we are used to. It was nothing to go round the ward on night-duty and find a few patients missing! They would return some hours later (often rather worse for wear) and smile on us as though they had done nothing unusual! Our batmen were an education to us in themselves. The majority of them had obviously been swinging from tree to tree in the jungles of India until only a few weeks previously. Several appeared to understand no known language, others had never even seen a white woman before, and were obviously reluctant to work for one. However, with perseverance, a little weeding-out, and the services of the much harassed Lance Naik in charge, we managed to get some idea of work into them.

Beyond our little patch of desert, where it grew increasingly ward, we had a mild sandstorm every evening for a month, the country was quite lovely. In May, the snow still lingered on the hills, yet wild tulips stood up out of it on the lower slopes. One could drive far out into rural districts that reminded one of home, little streams of ice cold water winding between green meadows decked with many of the English countryside flowers.

Teheran itself is a well laid out city, nice wide streets, with trees and buildings both pleasing to the eye and suitable to the climate. The shops unfortunately, were filled with the usual robbers; for instance, a pair of stockings one would blush to be seen giving away to a tramp, cost £3!

This extract suggests that as the war progressed military nurses were affected by the more insidious forms of militarisation. In addition to their officer status, battledress and protocol, they became inculcated with long-standing military attitudes. The British Empire was based on the notion that the British race was superior to many other races. Britain's imperial expansion had underpinned this opinion, and it was a theme perpetuated by military ideology. As nursing sisters were increasingly absorbed into the Army framework, their letters reflected a distinct shift in attitudes towards members of races other than their own. Though some accounts were favourable to different nationalities, others affirmed the military concept of social and racial hierarchy. Yet there were other occasions when nurses, such as those working in Persia, were confronted by cultures that were even more conscious of race and class than the British military hierarchy.

One nurse described the caste system among Indian ward orderlies in a letter to her matron:

The natives are divided into caste and class, and I believe it is the most difficult thing for anyone born, say, in the "sweeper" family to get into the "bearer" family. You meet it everywhere — in the wards we have orderlies (some English, some Anglo-Indian), who "do" for the patient; we have ward boys, who are the senior of the servants, and have everything to do with food and dusting the wards, ordering goods, etc. We have Beasties, who fetch and carry water and do the screening, and Sweepers, who sweep and white wash your walls, and clean the patients' boots, etc. Try and get the ward boy to fetch in a bowl of water, or an orderly to fetch a patient a dinner: he will feed the patient with it, but not fetch it. Ask the Beastie to pick up some fluff — he shouts for the ward boy, and he for the Sweeper, and they all shout together!

The intensification of the North African campaign meant that sisters were required to work extremely long hours in order to cope with the increasing numbers of casualties. However, their letters reveal that it was often difficult to persuade their Indian counterparts to do likewise.

Patients were expected at any moment, in unknown but certainly large numbers. From then on the whole personnel had hardly stopped working; pitching tents, unpacking and arranging stores and the multitude of other things inseparable from the starting of such organisations. There was an Indian officer commanding, two British medical officers, fifteen Anglo-Indian orderlies, sepoys and Indian followers. Food was eaten when and as they could get it, sleep was taken as a dire necessity. One disadvantage that we all suffered from for some time was that the unit had not done any work except training, since it was formed. Many of the sepoys were under the impression that army life was one long holiday and working eighteen hours a day and then not finished, was a rude awakening for them. This was complicated by the weather which was conducive to making them retire to the "godown" and stay there until the sun became warm again. The first patch of patients arrived as the first ward of tents was being erected and the neck and neck race between the arrival of patients and the erection of tents continued for about three weeks.

But while nurses were unable to instil the work ethic into some of their Indian ward orderlies, nearly all were impressed by the women who worked in the South African hospitals. Pietermaritzburg had established a 3,000-bedded hospital and began taking all the British wounded from North Africa and Egypt.

We had a railway siding of our own there. Hospital ships carrying wounded from the first "big push" in Egypt were brought down, disembarked at Durban, straight on to the hospital train along the docks, and brought thirty miles up country to us. On Christmas Eve 1942, we received 750 patients, 500 of whom were cot cases, some very badly wounded. In South Africa we collected all the sick from the Far East too, and there they waited until they were completely recovered and either returned to their units, or were sent home in a hospital ship. There were only two in that year, so our chief difficulty was to keep them happy and occupied during the time of waiting. One pathetic incident was two T.B. patients who were on the embarkation list, but died one hour before they were due to leave.

After six months in my medical ward I was given the orthopaedic ward, which was extremely heavy, with three fractured spines, amongst other serious cases. I never ceased to be surprised at the commonsense and efficiency of the South African VADs. They were mostly farmers' daughters, from far away inland, who had left their homes to volunteer. There was a large element of the Dutch (or Boer) amongst the nursing staff, and tact and diplomacy were needed in handling them, as their feelings towards the British still remains unchanged after all these years.

Christmas was magnificent with an abundance of everything. Parcels of all kinds kept coming to me from unknown donors, and the men lacked nothing; in fact, we all felt very sad when we remembered the privations of those at home. I did a great deal of occupational therapy amongst my patients, as the months were so long and tedious while they were waiting for their wounds to heal. The men did some excellent work of every description, including gardening (for which we won a rose bowl, in an inter-ward contest), wood carving, embroidery, and sculpture. We were entertained by all and sundry. The people could not do too much for us, welcoming us into their homes, on every occasion, and making real friends of us. The Services frequently gave entertainments in the Town Hall, which were very much appreciated by the townsfolk, who had very little in the way of distractions. Cinemas were excellent, in large air-conditioned buildings. The latest films were shown, but theatres were few and far between, and orchestral entertainment practically nil. There was a large convalescent camp accommodating 5,000 men about one mile down the road, where patients were transferred prior to returning to their units. A camp of about 5,000 Poles was nearby, whilst our next door neighbours were 5,000 Italian prisoners guarded by African natives.

There appeared to be a constant hive of activity in South African hospitals, and nurses had access to reasonable forms of entertainment. The desert experience was very different. One nurse working in the Middle East complained that:

The journey took just over nine weeks — a long and tedious one. We are in the desert and from my tent I look upon miles and miles of sand, with never a sight of a tree or a blade of grass. We have had one bad sandstorm and several minor ones during the last few weeks. You cannot imagine what they are like, you have to experience them to be able to believe how sand can penetrate. Life in the desert is a dreary affair, but the YWCA and the Red Cross are both good to us, especially the YWCA. They have opened a recreation hut for us and two of the sweetest women are in charge of it. I cannot speak too highly of what they have done in this land. At two different towns I have visited I have found branches, but the chief blessing is the little one in the desert. I wish I could give you a description of our life here, but censorship forbids.

Life in the desert had been boring for some time. Both the British and the Germans had been building up their strength and resources before commencing battle again. The British had staged an early counter-offensive in June 1941, code-named "Battleaxe", but this move had failed to gain ground. Subsequently, the British decided to reorganise the Eighth Army as the Western Desert Force under the guidance of Sir Claude Auchinleck. With the recent invasion of Russia, and the possibility of a German thrust through the Caucasus, strategic planning was also reassessed. Auchinleck chose to play a waiting game, and it was over four months before he launched an offensive against the German commander Erwin Rommel. Code-named "Crusader", the offensive was launched on 18 November and most of the action took place near Sidi Rezegh, south-east of Tobruk. Small combat units from both sides battled (sometimes on two fronts) until 27 November, by which time the

British XIII Corps had made substantial gains on the Sollum-Halfaya front, and other units had established links with the British garrison in Tobruk. Rommel decided to retreat, initially to the Gazala line and eventually to El Agheila.

Rommel was not defeated, however, and on 18 January 1942 he ordered a new offensive. After an intense period of fighting and substantial British losses, a lack of fuel and battle exhaustion brought both sides to a standstill on the Gazala line. A period of respite followed while equipment and supplies were replenished. Then, on 26 May, the Battle of Gazala began. Rommel had decided to launch his offensive before the British could take advantage of increased American supplies, and he was allowed temporary Luftwaffe cover to support this move. By 11 June the Germans had seized Bir Hacheim, and proceeded to Tobruk. The British Eighth Army began their retreat and during 20 and 21 June Tobruk was captured by Rommel's troops. However, instead of allowing the Luftwaffe to return to Sicily as previously arranged with Hitler, Rommel decided to press on towards Egypt and retained the services of the German Air Force. This turned out to be a major tactical error. Without the Luftwaffe in Sicily, German plans to invade Malta were indefinitely postponed.

The strategic importance of the island was obvious. Malta lay in the heart of the Mediterranean Sea and was a British possession. German and Italian supplies destined for North Africa were frequently intercepted by British warships and aircraft operating from bases in

Malta. Between the end of June 1942 and the beginning of January 1943, over 35 per cent of the supplies that were supposed to assist Rommel in his quest for supremacy in the desert failed to arrive. Not surprisingly, Malta endured constant and severe bombing raids throughout the Mediterranean conflict. Hitler had moved a German air corps to Sicily in readiness for an invasion of the island, which was planned for mid-July 1942. It was this contingent that was temporarily on loan to Rommel for his Libyan campaign. His decision to flout instructions and retain the Luftwaffe for further North African offensives effectively ruled out any invasion of Malta. Thus with the pressure lifted from the island, British warships were free to wreak havoc on German and Italian supply convoys. Subsequently, this sea warfare determined the course of the war.

Following the success of Rommel's forces in Tobruk, the British had retreated to the Alamein line. This position was close enough to the British base in Alexandria for Auchinleck and his troops to receive supplies. A railway line that ran from Alexandria to Alamein had been extended across Libya, and troops and supplies were transported with relative ease. Alamein, therefore, was chosen as an appropriate location for a defensive British stand. The first of the two main battles of El Alamein took place between 1 and 7 July 1942. The British were victorious and successfully defended Alamein by using highly mobile units. However, this victory was not fully recognised by Churchill. The British had defended Alamein but Rommel had advanced considerably, and Churchill chose to dwell on the fact that land had been conceded rather than on the successful defensive stand. As a result of Churchill's misconceptions about Alamein, Auchinleck was replaced by General Sir Harold Alexander and General Sir Bernard Law Montgomery.

The new officers of the Western Desert Force took some time to build up their resources, and subsequently they adopted much of the defensive strategy that had been recommended by their predecessor. Meanwhile, Rommel had decided that his next offensive would begin on 30 August. He then intended to push forward in an attempt to seize Egypt. British troops were expecting the attack and had made substantial defensive provisions for the event. The battle that ensued at Alam al Halfa Ridge resulted in a British victory. Rommel had experienced problems with fuel shortages and on 4 September he ordered a German withdrawal. Consequently, the British Eighth Army was in the ascendancy and assumed the offensive.

The second battle of Alamein lasted from 23 October to 4 November, and became a far more celebrated event than the first, although in many respects the result of the battle was a foregone conclusion. The United States had now mobilised and was a powerful British ally. The combined material superiority was unquestionable, and with Rommel's defence weakened by his own ill health the Germans were unable to do anything other than make one final stand. The losses were heavy on both sides but eventually Rommel retreated along the coast. Operation "Torch", which began on 8 November, sealed

Rommel's fate. Anglo-American forces landed in Algeria and Morocco and Rommel was caught between the Western Desert Force, which was advancing from Egypt, and the Anglo-American Force, which was in pursuit from Algeria. Rommel was able to fall back, and even to take command of a campaign in Tunisia. However, Anglo-American troops greatly outnumbered the remnants of Rommel's Panzer divisions, and by 4 February 1943 Libya had been totally taken over by the Anglo-American forces. By 12 May 1943 the war in the desert was virtually over and 240,000 German and Italian soldiers were captured.

The battle for supremacy in the desert had been a long struggle and one that largely determined the course of the war. Matron Cocking described the scene in Benghazi once the fighting had subsided:

I had seen a few ancient ruins by this time but the shell of Benghazi was the first modern one I had encountered. There was scarcely an undamaged building standing, but the hospital buildings, shared by an RAF hospital and ourselves, were untouched. We lived in one wing of the hospital to start with, as the bungalows we occupied later were then unfit for habitation, having been badly knocked about. The place was filthy and the sisters started straight away to clean it up. Unluckily, two of them dropped a marble table on their feet, breaking some bones; but after a few days they were getting about quite nicely in plaster and walking irons.

Most of us were in Benghazi for four months and I, for one, shall find it hard to forget. The countryside with its carpet of flowers, blue, red and gold stretching for miles on either side, the blue lagoon where we bathed, the gold of the wattle trees, the little white homesteads planted by Mussolini (built exactly to a pattern, as he would have liked all men to be). All so peaceful, 'til one noticed the wrecks of cars, tanks, lorries and aeroplanes at intervals upon the wayside, grim reminders of the reason for our being here.

There is another reason why we shall not forget Benghazi. It is because of the help and comradeship so freely offered to us by men of all ranks in the units amongst whom we worked. We reached Tripoli early in June and were attached pro temp to no. 48 General Hospital. Except for lecturing and examining the orderlies, there was not much to do during our period of waiting. Towards the end of our stay, as convoys started coming in to no. 48 General Hospital, our sisters were able to lend a hand there.

His Majesty, King George VI paid a visit to Tripoli while we were there, and we were present when he inspected 48 General Hospital. His visit meant a great deal to everyone, especially the men. At the same time, we were greatly relieved to hear that he had arrived home again in safety. Towards the end of July, our men left for Sicily. One week later, we embarked on a hospital ship and followed them.

Desert warfare had consisted of a series of military campaigns involving thousands of troops. Consequently, the North African battlefields had provided an excellent testing ground for new medical technology, including the introduction of a new "wonder drug". Penicillin was to revolutionise medical treatment and although plentiful supplies were not available until later in the war, the impact of the drug was enormous. Thousands of soldiers were saved from the horrors of gas-gangrene and other bacterial infections that had been rampant in previous conflicts. The drug was also used for the treatment of venereal disease as one nurse recalled: "The first time (it was very delicate), I think we'd better not say it, because it was used for the V.D.s, the Gonorrheas, because it was supposed to have an instant effect and they wanted every man back ready for fighting."

The Prime Minister also benefited from the drug. In the December of 1943, during a visit to the Eighth Army in North Africa, Churchill developed pneumonia and received penicillin to combat the illness. His successful recovery was proof positive that the drug could work miracles.

The days of administering hot poultices and sponge baths were over, and in some instances good old-fashioned nursing care was rendered superfluous. As Monica Baly remembered, "No longer was the doctor saying, 'I can't do anything, but nursing will do a great deal'. We had now got to the stage when it appeared as if nursing was not doing very much. The patients got better whether they were nursed or not." Doctors pointed out, however, that any form of chemotherapy (that is, treatment using drugs of any sort, and not just the treatment of cancer, with which the term chemotherapy is nowadays most often associated) could not entirely rule out the need for surgical intervention in the treatment of battle injuries. Nevertheless, penicillin was quickly hailed as a "miracle drug" and used to facilitate surgical techniques. Reporting on the new medical techniques that could be assisted by its use, the medical and nursing press explained that:

In this war there have been two quite different approaches to the application of chemotherapeutic agents to military surgery. The first would utilise these agents to permit delay in wound surgery and minimise the incision of tissue destroyed by the missile. The second employs chemotherapy to extend the scope of surgery and achieve a perfection in results previously considered impossible.

The latter policy has guided the surgery of the Mediterranean theatre. To reiterate the axiom that penicillin is not a substitute for surgery is not enough. Every surgeon must learn that chemotherapy opens new and startling possibilities in wound management. To fully realise the potentialities of reparative surgery requires the introduction of a new concept in the organisation of military surgery. Four to ten days is the "golden period" during which time wounds must be closed, fractures reduced, retained missiles removed and any other procedure to prevent or abort infection must be carried out.

Failure to take cognisance of the potentialities of early reparative surgery at the base in the future plans and operations will be as glaring an omission as a failure to plan for the removal of the wounded from the field of battle.

Military medical teams were no longer concerned merely with saving lives; they now expected their patients to make a full recovery and, more often than not, they did. Nurses became accustomed to administering the foul-smelling yellow substance every four hours, and to the rapid recovery of patients who had, hitherto, been expected to die. But it was some time before nurses were able to carve out a new niche for nursing care. Their professional status was already under threat, and to some extent the introduction of penicillin compounded matters. How were nurses able to justify their professional status when one drug could undermine most of their traditional nursing techniques?

The implementation of the 1943 Nurses Act, the use of cadet nurses, and the lack of trained staff had already reduced professional status within the civilian nursing sector. However, beleaguered by VAD status problems since the outbreak of war, military nurses were now confronted with a drug that had the ability to undermine seriously their fields of nursing practice. It is possible, for instance, that the news of penicillin influenced the government's decision to restrict the intake of experienced civilian nurses into the military from 1943 onwards. Government officials may have taken the view that experienced nurses were no longer needed in the military because of the immense improvements effected in patients treated by the drug. The decision was taken, ostensibly, because the civilian sector was suffering from a severe shortage of experienced registered nurses. But the restrictions, which allowed only newly qualified nurses to join up, could not have come at a worse time. With the Germans retreating from North Africa, the tide of the war had changed. Britain was preparing to fight on a second front and casualties were expected in unprecedented numbers.

CHAPTER
FIVE

Returning to Europe

The restrictions imposed on the recruitment of registered nurses into the armed forces caused severe nursing shortages. At times, a force of 2,000 QAs were nursing, under stress, extra beds to the tune of 12,000. Given that huge numbers of casualties were expected in forthcoming military campaigns, the military VAD nursing problems needed to be resolved as a matter of urgency. The confused background of events that had led to disputes, bad feeling, and a sense of injustice among military registered nurses and male RAMC orderlies alike were described by Dame Katherine Jones:

In 1939 the VADs were embodied under precisely the same conditions as the ATS and the FANYs, a fact which is often forgotten. Many difficulties of accommodation and messing arose with all these new women recruits, due entirely to our general unpreparedness for war.

In the case of the VADs with a powerful voluntary organisation behind them and their discomforts, changes were demanded and made in 1940, which resulted in the granting of a series of privileges for the nursing members only, so substantial as to give rise in some quarters to the statement that they enjoyed officer status (in some respects they did, but off-duty only) without the rank or justification of officer responsibilities.

They also gave rise to anomalies vis-à-vis the grade 2 non-nursing VADs (often trained masseuses, dispensers, radiographers, cooks, clerks, etc.) and the ATS which finally precipitated an Army Council proposal for the assimilation of the VADs in the ATS.

However, although Dame Katherine's concerns over VAD privileges were prompted by the possible blurring of distinctions between registered and non-registered nurses, the Army Council proposals were initiated by more practical considerations. VAD nurses had refused to undertake the more menial nursing tasks, and had offloaded them onto the male RAMC orderlies. The Army Council had recognised that as more RAMC orderlies were required to work on the frontline there would be no one left behind to undertake these menial tasks. This was by far the most important reason for suggesting that VADs should become part of the ATS. Nevertheless, there were other considerations.

The Army claimed that the existing organisational structure was inefficient and did not fully utilise man and woman power. There was some justification for this claim. A number of VADs were capable of undergoing training courses that would equip them for a career in nursing once the war was over. But, under the existing scheme, VADs were unable to take advantage of training opportunities regardless of their individual abilities. Under the new Army Council proposals, VADs would be incorporated into the ATS and be eligible for advancement up to the rank of warrant officer. It was suggested that the new VAD branch of the ATS would be organised through the ATS record office, as the new branch would form an integral part of the ATS and not of the RAMC. The Army proposals, however, were not merely designed to resolve strategic status issues and encourage VAD training: the proposals made provision for the Army to dispense with the services of the VAD Council. There were, therefore, sound economic reasons for the Army takeover bid, since Army funds would no longer be awarded to the VAD Council or to the VAD county controllers. The Army would also acquire a substantial nursing force to direct at will.

There were, nonetheless, important political problems associated with the Army takeover bid. Army officials had not, for example, considered the wider implications of a merger between VAD and ATS personnel. The proposals, if accepted, clearly compromised the position of the British Red Cross within the international arena. Red Cross principles were based overwhelmingly on the concept of political neutrality. There was a very real danger that international observers may have viewed a military takeover of the voluntary nursing services as the thin end of the wedge. If the military could take over Red Cross nursing services, then why not their communications and administration networks? The war organisation of the British Red Cross and the Order of St

John "found it necessary to be continuously vigilant in the maintenance of the principles of Red Cross independence, neutrality and impartiality, including the unique position of the society in relation to general wartime charitable endeavour. It was imperative not to endanger privileges of the International Red Cross Committee or to give an enemy power an excuse to question the impartiality of any Red Cross service."

Red Cross organisations in any country were not supposed to be under the direction of individual governments, though there is considerable evidence to suggest that this condition was breached in Germany. Independence of humanitarian action was crucial to the work of the Red Cross and the Order of St John. The war organisation of these voluntary bodies had outlined their purpose as follows: "To ameliorate the conditions of the wounded and the sick in armies in the field. To furnish aid to the sick and wounded, to all prisoners of war, and civilians needing relief as a result of enemy action".

The Red Cross and the Order of St John had a long-established tradition of training first-aiders and nursing aids for wartime service, and nurses working with these voluntary organisations were outraged at the idea of being incorporated into the ATS. There was also considerable opposition from the voluntary organisations concerned. Given the overall shortage of medical personnel, the armed forces could not afford to "get on the wrong side" of these organisations. A forced takeover of voluntary nurses was not likely to foster good relationships between state and voluntary medical services. Therefore, for the sake of maintaining some semblance of "goodwill", the proposed merger was rejected. As Dame Katherine explained: "The proposal evoked protests and was only withdrawn after the Elliot Interdepartmental Committee had recommended a compromise that the conditions of service of VADs be brought into line with all other women in the army (and the male RAMC) who were performing comparable duties, in fact a reversion to the conditions which had been agreed by all parties in 1939."

The VAD Council was substituted with a standing committee that incorporated the Council of Territorial Associations, along with representatives from the various voluntary organisations. The problems of VAD task allocation had, at long last, been resolved and the Army could move RAMC orderlies to the frontline in greater numbers. The British and American forces, having captured North Africa, were now planning to invade Sicily.

The logic behind the decision to invade Sicily was quite simple. Churchill believed that an invasion of this triangular-shaped Mediterranean island would have important strategic consequences. An invasion would strengthen British maritime operations and communications in this area, take some of the heat off Russia, which had been embroiled in intense fighting with the Germans since 1941, and weaken the political relationship between Italy and Germany.

Operation "Husky" was essentially an amphibious operation that began on the night of 9 July 1943. The weather was appalling and the landings were hampered by strong winds. Montgomery and the British Eighth

Army landed on the south-east coast, and the American General George Patton with the American Seventh Army landed on the east coast. Both subsequently became involved in a race towards Messina. By dawn on 11 July the division had landed and had met very little in the way of enemy resistance. Later in the morning, however, both Italian and German aircraft began to scour the skies, picking out British and American shipping vessels at random. Later still, at 3 o'clock in the afternoon, intense fighting began as the German commander Hermann Goring staged a counter-attack against the land-borne troops. Eventually an American battalion managed to ward off the Germans, though not before sustaining heavy casualties.

On 11 July the Italians and Germans staged a more earnest counter-attack at Gela. Under severe pressure from the Italian 33rd and 34th Regiments, advancing from the north-west, and the German Panzergrenadiers, advancing from the north-east, the Americans retreated. With the Germans only four miles away from Gela, and the Italians only one mile away, the Americans needed to take drastic action. With the help of considerable naval gunfire, Patton and the 1st Division managed to halt the enemy advance. Although the Panzers had been within 500 yards of the shoreline by midday, the battle had finished. Both the Germans and Italians had to beat a hasty retreat in the face of combined naval and artillery gunfire.

British and American troops assessed their gains before advancing, and by 15 July they had captured the south-east part of the island. As they pushed forward across the Catania Plain, the British encountered strong German resistance. But from this point on it appeared that neither Montgomery nor Patton acted on direct orders from their respective headquarters. Instead, they embarked on their own personal and very competitive military strategies. Montgomery had instructed the Canadian forces to break away and make a left arc around Mount Etna. Patton, meanwhile, infuriated by Montgomery's action, decided to go it alone across Sicily. Firstly, he created a provisional corps that advanced across western Sicily and, secondly, he instructed his 1st and 45th Divisions to drive across Sicily towards the north coast. On 22 July Palermo was captured and the 1st and 45th Divisions managed to reach the north coast by 23 July.

Montgomery and the Eighth Army had secured at least half of the Catania Plain by 23 July, but had sustained severe casualties in the process. Clearly, both German and Italian forces had planned to evacuate their troops from Sicily at some point, but they intended to hold out for as long as possible and inflict considerable damage on British and American troops. Between 23 July and 10 August both sides battled fiercely before the German High Command decided to initiate the evacuation of troops in order to save valuable manpower. Some troops had, in fact, retreated to Italy much sooner, particularly those who were involved in the struggle for Napoli. The Germans did stage a rearguard action at Brolo on 11 August and almost managed to isolate the 2nd Battalion of the 30th Infantry Regiment. Following a period of twenty-nine hours of intense fighting and aerial bombardment, the remainder of the regiment arrived and relieved the situation.

Meanwhile, Montgomery was still battling it out with Goring's troops near Mount Etna. Eventually, the Germans lost their grip on 13 August under the combined pressure of the Canadian and American 9th Divisions and the British 78th Division. Thus began the race to Messina, which Patton won on 17 August. The American general arrived just three hours before his rival Montgomery. But despite the intense fighting and the remarkable offensive campaigns, the Germans and Italians still managed successfully to evacuate over 102,000 men, 9,827 vehicles, 134 pieces of artillery and 2,000 tons of ammunition, all of which could be used by the German forces intent on defending Italy.

Apart from the failure of Allied forces to prevent the German evacuation, there was also a failure to provide adequate care for the casualties in Sicily. A report written after the event by Colonel Atkins claimed that the medical arrangements for Operation "Husky" were not all that they should have been: "Medical Branch Force cannot be expected to take for granted that all the arrangements on ships are satisfactory; and administrative measures should be taken on a high level to ensure that medical force have the right to inspect all ships to ensure that arrangements and equipment are satisfactory. Operation 'Husky' showed that a number of these ships had most unsatisfactory medical arrangements."

But if medical arrangements were less than adequate and the Allies had not entirely succeeded with their objectives, at least some comfort could be found on the political front. The collapse of Sicily confirmed Italian suspicions that to continue to wage war against the combined might of British and American troops was a foolish endeavour. The King of Italy had already ousted Mussolini from power on 26 July, and Pietro Badoglio, as the Italian prime minister, had begun secret negotiations with Britain and America in an attempt to reach an armistice.

As Churchill had expected, the capture of Sicily had weakened the Italian resolve. The venture had also clarified British and American strategy in the Mediterranean. They had, however, sustained heavy losses: at least 20,000 men compared to 12,000 on the German side. There were also a considerable number of casualties, many of whom were victims of land mines. For military nurses, though, Sicily provided a welcome change from the oppressive heat of the North African desert, and in some areas battle casualties were few. As Matron Cocking wrote of her time in Syracuse:

We could hardly get away from the illusion that we were on a camping holiday. Tentage was short, so our mess tent was provided by a huge lotus tree, which served the purpose just as well, and was far more picturesque. Blackout was very severe on account of Jerry's fondness for "popping over", so we could not show a light even in our tents. Brains were racked for means to break the monotony of the dark hours, after 8p.m. One of the sisters had a gramophone with which she occasionally gave gramophone recitals, working it in the dark. The Colonel organized a series of talks on different subjects by various people. All were invited to listen and join in the discussion after.

It was in the orchard that our unit newspaper, *Odyssey*, was born. Articles of interest covering a wide range of subjects, poetry, criticisms, witticisms, sketches were asked for and received from both staff and patients. Since that time, each Sunday morning a copy has been set up in a prominent position, where it could be read by all. The Sicilians, like the Italians, were great thieves, and the men missed many things from their tents. The sisters lost nothing, thanks to the good offices of "Socks". Always a good watchdog, he bore a great hatred towards the Italians. After he relieved one man of a piece of his trousers, I decided to muzzle him, as I was afraid of him hurting a child. He did not mind this much, and as he still looked, and sounded ferocious, unwanted visitors kept their distance.

The sisters were not able to enjoy the holiday camp atmosphere for long. Soon casualties began pouring into the casualty clearing stations and mobile medical units. Matron Cocking continued:

Four weeks after our arrival, the Colonel told me at 6p.m. one evening that he had received orders for us to move with the greatest speed possible. Our patients were evacuated by 10a.m. the next day. By the same time the day after, our entire equipment had been loaded, and it and us were in lorries on the road to our next destination.

We arrived at Giarre, a small town under the shadow of Mount Etna, after darkness had fallen. We now found ourselves in an old school building, which I trust had been more successful in its teaching than it had in its sanitary arrangements! We spent one night in what were later wards. Next morning, I went flat hunting in town with the Colonel and found two, quite near together, that made quite a suitable mess. We also found a flat, not far from the main building, that made an excellent sick officers' and sisters' hospital.

Next day, while we were still unloading the hospital equipment, the patients started to arrive. Here, we received patients that had come more or less directly from the battlefields. We were wearing white, as the local women laundered well for us. One morning I started to hear, from the lines of ambulances bringing in the wounded, cries of "Look, look! Do you see that? A real English nurse!"

We were nearly always full here, often overflowing. We had a neuro-surgical and a facial-maxillary team attached to us and the work was very interesting. The sad part was that we could only keep our patients for so short a time; all except the dangerously ill had to go on as soon as possible, to make room for others. Rows of patients were often waiting on stretchers to go out as others were coming in.

The introduction of facial-maxillary units near to the frontline was a pioneering military medical innovation. During the First World War, very little attention was paid to the men who sustained facial injuries. They were expected to walk to the casualty clearance stations unaided and most died from shock as a result. The previously high mortality rate from facial wounds was reduced dramatically during the Second World War as highly mobile units treated facial wounds as a matter of urgency.

Our little unit nipped about and kept as close as possible so that the men, as soon as they were wounded, got treatment on the spot. And we had a fantastically high record of recovery. It was a wonderful unit to work for. I was absolutely amazed at what could be done. With the men whose faces had been burned off, over several operations the flesh and the skin was replaced, noses were swung down in a flap from the forehead, even being so careful as to include a tiny edge of the hair bearing skin where it would normally meet the forehead. This was turned round into this new nose to be tucked inside the nostril so that there were hairs in the nostrils.

There were also new treatments for burns. Burns were a particular problem for pilots, and the nurses in the PMRAFNS could spend up to eight hours dressing serious wounds. Originally, the treatment for burns had been the application of tannic acid, a procedure that resulted in considerable tissue damage. However, in July 1940 this procedure was abandoned in favour of saline infusions and "tulle gras" dressings. Such was the experimentation in the treatment of burns that a "guinea pig" club was established in 1942, along with numerous specialist burns units.

Progress in chest surgery was another feature of the Italian campaign. In 1945 the *British Journal of Nursing* reported that:

Military surgeons are focusing attention on the restoration of full lung function rather than the mere prevention of empyema in chest wounds — an important advance in thoracic surgery which is reflected in the surprisingly high number of chest cases returned to duty in the Italian campaign. Out of 320 men admitted to one general hospital with penetrating chest wounds, 225 either returned to duty or were prevented from doing so by other injuries. Only 54 developed empyema. Of these, it was felt that five might require further surgery. And only two deaths in the group were attributable to chest wounds.

There had also been considerable experimentation with regard to paratroops, their medical problems and their safety. As the Director of the British Medical Services proclaimed:

A variety of helmets, spine pads, boots and bandages were tried out with a view to discovering methods of preventing injury to the brain, spinal column and lower limbs, which were found to be the most frequent sites of injury. For months, tests to recognise liability to air-sickness, which entailed swinging all new intake in horizontal swings for 20 minutes, were carried out. Prolonged trials of a variety of drugs to prevent air-sickness were also indulged in and hundreds of shattered, retching, but undaunted Airborne troops co-operated in carrying out these tests with amazing cheerfulness and willingness. The whole of the intake was tested for colour blindness. Rigorous ration trials were carried out with a view to ascertaining the lightest and least bulky ration which could be made available for the Airborne forces. Various types of clothing and equipment, considered necessary for Airborne troops, were tested and reported on.

In the end, it has been found that the questions of air-sickness, injury, refusals, in effect preventable wastage, is largely bound up with the correct selection of officers and men. Every officer and man is encouraged to submit recommendations and suggestions and to report on any defects in organisation or equipment. As a result, it has been possible to build up a Medical Service which is efficient and which has gained the complete confidence of the combatant troops.

It has been said that one of the most striking features of British Airborne Divisions is the high esteem in which their medical services are held by the fighting troops and the active co-operation with them which is always present. Further advances can and will be made, but the officers and men who were the pioneers of Airborne Medical Services have at least laid a sound foundation on which a Medical Service of great potentialities can be built, and in spite of disappointments and failures they can feel that their labour was not entirely in vain.

Some of the earlier disappointments of the Airborne Medical Services centred on the very real problems of weight and size limitations. Specialist equipment was therefore devised, which included:

The folding airborne stretcher, collapsible wheeled stretcher carriage. Light folding trestles, folding suspension bar, airborne operating table, plasma containers for dropping by parachute, insulated blood containers and "Don" and "Sugar" packs. The "Don" packs contain sufficient dressings, drugs, medical comforts, etc., for 20 patients, while the "Sugar" pack is sufficient for resupply for 10 surgical cases in the operating theatre.

The methods by which this equipment is taken into action are:

On the man — in the case of parachute troops, in a kit bag tied to the leg and fitted with a quick release which allows the man to detach the bag from the leg while in the air, the bag then remaining suspended from his belt. In the case of Air Landing Troops, in haversacks or large pack of the web equipment.

* * *

In containers dropped on parachutes from the bomb racks.

In airborne panniers dropped on parachutes and thrown out of the door of the aircraft.

In gliders — in this case the medical stores are loaded in jeeps and trailers, and on landing can be conveyed to where they are required.

The Director of the British Medical Services issued a prudent warning with regard to gliders, however, stating that:

Gliders and containers unfortunately do not always land where they are intended, and it is therefore laid down as a principle in the airborne medical services, that the basic equipment, both for glider and parachute personnel, must be in loads with which the men themselves can land and march. This necessitates the careful selection of essential medical equipment and the packing of it into suitable bundles and packs.

As the Airborne Medical Services confronted their transportation problems new techniques in medical care were yet again proving their worth on the battlefield. Nurses who worked with the mobile medical units were usually the nearest to the frontline. This policy ensured that treatment was administered as soon as possible. The larger hospital units were also near the frontline but were not as mobile and, as a consequence of long-term aerial bombardment, it became more and more difficult to find adequate accommodation, both for the staff and their patients.

That evening, Captain Brewer took me along to the ADMS who said he had found an ideal mess for us, a 16th century villa, dating back to the Medici family. It was then occupied by naval personnel and we went round for the men to inspect it, it being considered too dirty for my feminine eyes to gaze upon! As I sat in the car, two sailors leaned confidentially over the balcony: "Hey, Miss! Don't you let them put you in 'ere. There's a corpse under that gateway, and it smells like it!" They were perfectly right! Nevertheless, by the time that had been removed, a roof or two that had been shattered by bombs replaced, the house thoroughly cleaned, disinfected and cleared of appalling rubbish, it was really quite delightful. We were left with sufficient furniture by the owner to be very comfortable. A few of the sisters joined me in a few days and soon had everything ready for the others when they moved up with the unit.

We stayed at Messina our usual three to four weeks. The work was quite satisfying, and as we were not dealing with such numbers as at Giarre, we were able to keep our patients longer. We received quite a number of enterics and diphtherias as well as our fair share of malarias. Battle casualties were few.

The view from the hospital was lovely. It faced directly across the straits of Messina. You felt you only had to give a jump to land over in Italy. The water was fascinating to watch. Convoys would pass to and fro along the straits, transports would cross continuously and once a whole fleet of amphibians crossed over, looking for all the world like a row of ducks crossing the village pond. Amongst all these, the little sailing boats tacked to and fro. On a day early in October, having handed over to a field hospital, we too passed over to the other side and the Sicilian Episode was over.

The Anglo-American invasion of Italy began on 3 September, and their troops were landed on the west coast of Italy, at Salerno, on 9 September. By clinging to the coastline they initially managed to avoid many of the German attempts to stem their advance. The day before the Salerno landing Italy surrendered, and on 13 October declared war on Germany. By early October Naples had fallen to the Anglo-American forces and they pushed northwards. They were soon thwarted by German troops at the Abbey of Monte Cassino, however, the centre of what Hitler had named the Gustav line. After months of land fighting and aerial bombing, during which the abbey itself and many art treasures were destroyed, Anglo-American troops were dropped behind the Gustav line in January 1944. But they did not manage to actually breach the line until May 1944. Rome was captured by the Anglo-Americans on 5 June. The intense battles had, not surprisingly, taken their toll on the Italian countryside and people. As Monica Baly, working with the RAF, remembered:

> The awful thing, the thing that I remember very very well was: they used to come to the dustbins and they used to pick out everything that we had thrown out in the way of food, and carry it away in pots. Because they were starving poor things.
>
> We took over the hospital at Pontio, which had been left by the retreating Germans who had kindly blown up the sewers, and I have never seen anything quite so desolate as southern Italy. It really did upset me. It was so utterly devastated. You now really saw what war did. This had been fought over by the Italians, fought over by the Germans, fought over by the Americans, the Americans had bombed it to kingdom come, and we took over this shell of a hospital. I have never been so cold in all my life. We had a bombed house with no windows in it for the sisters' sleeping quarters, so we slept on our camp beds with every bit of blanket we could find.

Another nurse recalled the cold for other reasons: "In Italy it was very cold at night. When we were on night duty we had to wear battledress and, just going round with hurricane lamps, I was bending over a patient one night just to enquire how he was and, of course, poor chap, he was asleep. He came to and he must have thought I was a German. He screamed the place down and I had to pacify him."

Matron Cocking remembered the cold, and also the utter confusion of her arrival in Italy, and the problems of finding accommodation:

On Monday, 4th of October 1943 we came to Reggio in Italy. Here we waited for a few days before we entrained as some bridges had been damaged and were being repaired. We then went on to Bari, but did not function as a hospital, owing to a lack of accommodation. Here we found hairdressers, tailors, cleaners and hat renovators, of whom we were all in sad need. We found we could not buy any new materials, but it was a joy even to have one's old garments spruced up.

We were beginning to think of ourselves as the "unwanted unit", when, in November, orders came for the Advance Party to proceed to Santa Maria, on the further side of Italy. As I found I could stay at 92 General Hospital in Naples I went with it. We travelled by truck, up by Foggia and across the Apennines to Naples, a delightful run. We reached the town after dark and found that they kept their blackout only too well! We spent hours trying to find our headquarters. Forms kept looming out of the darkness and a Yankee voice would say, "Say pal! Where you going?" To which we would sadly reply, "We only wish we knew!" Once we found HQ our troubles were over.

Next day, Major Craik and I were taken over to Santa Maria to see the prison, our proposed future residence. It was still functioning as an Italian gaol and I can't say more than that it was all you would imagine an Italian gaol to be! So that was written off! Every day for a week we toured the surrounding district in search of a suitable site. We went over schools, monasteries, wine factories and finally a castle. Wherever we went, people were very kind to us, but I had no idea it could have been so difficult to find us a corner in which to work. We had great hopes of our castle, a very fascinating one, spacious, more or less adaptable and in lovely surroundings, but it was decreed that we were to go to an old Italian military hospital at Nocera. This was being held in readiness for no. 103 General Hospital and we were sent to function there until they were ready to take over. Two days later we joined the rest of our unit at Nocera and started work immediately to relieve the pressure in other hospitals. We had two 100 bedded expansions from no. 104 General Hospital attached to us here and found that we needed all the beds we could get.

The mess buildings were not completed, so we had to live in one wing of the hospital buildings. The wards, when we got them cleaned and in working order, were quite nice, lofty and spacious. The roofs were in bad repair and were in the process of being mended when we arrived. As the rainy season arrived at the same time, we spent the first week or two moving the beds to avoid a waterfall and arranging bowls to catch the drips! There were no actual baths, but plenty of showers and the hot water system worked! Sanitary arrangements — as usual!

Throughout the war it appeared that bombers on both sides of the conflict would not deliberately bomb hospital buildings. It was usual, therefore, to find that although ancient monuments and other buildings were virtually obliterated, hospitals were left relatively intact. However, they were frequently not of the standard to which British military nurses were accustomed. Even the sturdy buildings that were taken over and used as hospitals sometimes left a lot to be desired, and it was not unusual for nurses to call on the services of some of the fitter patients in an attempt to improve surroundings, as Matron Cocking explains:

103 General Hospital began to arrive over Christmas and on New Year's Eve we found ourselves on the way to Pontycagniano, in the teeth of a howling gale. This time we were going to an old Italian barracks which were being evacuated by the RAF. The latter were very good to us, had a blazing log fire in our mess room to greet us, and had even laid on a New Year's Eve party to revive our dampened spirits. Our mess room had evidently been the one used by Italian officers. It had a good floor and fireplace, a bar in one corner and quite a serviceable kitchen attached. Our sleeping quarters were also satisfactory.

The wards were not so good. The floors were of brick, very uneven, and felt damp. Only a few had stoves and fireplaces built in and it took a little time for valor stoves to make any impression. As usual, our patients followed hard upon our heels, and, to our joy, we discovered some bricklayers amongst them. Discovering some unused bricks lying about outside, they soon had fireplaces up in all the most serious wards. The REs worked very hard, putting in lighting, making a workable operating theatre, more or less satisfactory latrines and wash houses, even a laundry! Here our brooms gave out and we were unable to get replacements. For a time we were using twigs bound together till some Americans came to the rescue and gave us a supply of stout witch-brooms.

I don't know who was responsible for labelling Italy "sunny", but he certainly could not have been here in the winter months! How it rained! What was later the hospital cookhouse was, on our arrival, a miniature farmyard. The cooks had to function more or less in the open, while it poured "cats and dogs" and an icy wind blew — yet I never knew the food to suffer.

As we were very near the original landing beaches, the neighbourhood was well mined and, as at Giarre, one could not venture off the beaten track. We admitted a lot of mine casualties during our early days, quite a number being local children. We also received many patients suffering from diphtheria, which appears to be a common infection in these parts. We were kept reasonably busy, and as the weather improved, the surroundings began to look a little less grim! The patients were really marvellous. It was almost unheard of to hear a complaint; they were always cheery, always ready to help.

Military nurses in Italy were kept busy for some time. Even though Rome had been captured on 5 June 1944 the fighting continued for another eleven months as the Anglo-American troops gradually pushed northwards. Elsewhere, events in Russia had reached a turning-point. The Soviet counter-blows to the German invasion of 1941 had taken some time to bear fruit. Throughout 1941 and most of 1942 the Red Army was uncoordinated and inexperienced in military strategy. By the end of 1942, having waged a successful war of attrition against the Germans, the Red Army began to feel its feet. The Stalingrad counter-offensive began on 19 November 1942 and, after bitter fighting, on 2 February 1943 German forces surrendered Stalingrad. This surrender had a huge impact on the morale of the Red Army and dealt a severe blow to the Germans. Until this point, many people in Germany had believed in the "invincibility" of the German Army. Any minor defeats were carefully hidden by propaganda, but the Stalingrad defeat was too severe to hide from the German public. Too many Germans had been captured or killed in the conflict. It was impossible, therefore, for the German population to pretend that Stalingrad had been anything other than an unmitigated disaster.

The Soviet strategy for 1943 was based on a two-pronged approach. First, the Red Army intended to adopt deep defensive lines at Kursk and gradually reduce the number of enemy tanks, then to launch an immensely powerful offensive that would leave the German forces stunned and annihilated. Even before the plans for the Kursk battle had been completed troops had begun to take up positions. Within a few weeks, over a million troops were resident inside Kursk. Over 400,000 mines had been laid on the central front and trenches were constructed over a span of 3,000 miles. Airfields to the tune of 150 were built, in addition to the numerous "dummy" airfields that were created to confuse the enemy. On 5 July 1943 the Battle of Kursk began, and it has since been recognised by many historians as the most significant battle of the entire war. Richard Overy supports this view in his book *Why the Allies Won*:

> Soviet success at Kursk, with so much at stake, was the most important single victory of the war. It ranks with the great setpiece battles of the past — Sedan in 1870, and Borodino, Leipzig and Waterloo from the age of Napoleon. It was the point at which the initiative passed to the Soviet side. German forces were certainly capable of a sustained and effective defence as they retreated westwards; but they were now too weakened and overstretched to inflict a decisive defeat on their enemy.

The Soviet successes at Stalingrad and Kursk determined the fortunes of the remainder of the war. The losses on the Soviet side were horrendous. Their leader, Stalin, never revealed the exact cost in human lives. Soldiers who were killed or wounded in the conflicts were referred to as the "countless" citizens who had died and suffered for "Mother Russia". It is estimated, however, that at least 20 million Russians did lose their lives. Between August and December 1943 the German front to the east was forced to retreat, and one by one Soviet cities were reclaimed. Nevertheless, there was still a considerable amount of territory left to be reclaimed in order to oust the Germans from Russia completely. On 28 November Stalin met with his allies Churchill and Roosevelt in Teheran to decide overall strategy. During their conference, Stalin was presented with a "sword of honour", a gift from the British King George VI, in recognition of the Russian victory at Stalingrad. The Red Army had clearly inflicted immense damage on the German forces. However, as the fighting continued, Stalin argued, as he had done on previous occasions, for the introduction of a "second front". In response, both Churchill and Roosevelt assured him that an attack on Europe would be launched in the spring of the following year. Thus began the preparations for Operation "Overlord".

CHAPTER
SIX

Face to Face with the Enemy

As the preparations began for Operation "Overlord" (more commonly remembered as the D-Day landings), the military nursing shortages became more apparent. British military nurses were still suffering from the recruiting restrictions that had been imposed in 1943. The problem for American military nurses was quite different. Whereas in Britain there had been a deluge of nurses who had wanted to join up, and hence the subsequent restrictions on military intake, in America nurses quite simply did not want to join up at all. The situation became so dire that eleven American hospital units were sent overseas without their complement of nurses, and over 1,000 American Army nurses were hospitalised, suffering from exhaustion. Despite intensive recruitment campaigns, American women did not respond. It was estimated that at least 50,000 nurses would be needed to assist the American troops in the D-Day operations and the deficit was at least 10,000. Recruitment drives had brought in only an extra 2,000 nurses.

Eventually, President Roosevelt made an emotional and patriotic plea to Congress for help:

It is tragic that the gallant women who have volunteered for service as nurses should be so overworked. It is tragic that our wounded men should ever want for the best possible nursing care. The inability to get the needed nurses for the Army is not due to any shortage of nurses. Two hundred and eighty thousand registered nurses are now practising in this country. It has been estimated by the War Manpower Commission that 27,000 additional nurses could be made available to the armed forces without interfering too seriously with the needs of the civilian population for nurses.

Since volunteering has not produced the number of nurses required, I urge that the Selective Service Act be amended to provide for the induction of nurses into the armed forces. The need is too pressing to await the outcome of further efforts at recruiting. The care and treatment given to our wounded and sick soldiers has been the best known to medical science. Those standards must be maintained at all costs. We cannot tolerate a lowering of them by failure to provide adequate nursing for the brave men who stand desperately in need of it.

Indeed, an ironic situation had emerged, whereby the British were imposing restrictions on nurses entering the services and the Americans were considering imposing a draft to force nurses to enter the services. To some extent the British situation was relieved by Commonwealth nurses, but the American situation had no such respite. With troops in the Far East, in addition to those preparing for D-Day, their medical services were stretched to breaking point.

Problems of medical back-up were not the only difficulties confronting the Anglo-American alliance. For at least two years the countries had disagreed on military strategy. Churchill had preferred to wage war on the periphery of Europe and to pursue a policy of dispersal, hoping that the enemy would be worn down and substantially weakened before attempting any full-on assault. Eisenhower preferred a full-scale invasion of Europe and an attack at the earliest opportunity. Despite his preferences, however, Churchill was effectively scuppered during the November conference with Eisenhower and Stalin, when it was clear that the Russian leader gave wholehearted support to the American plan.

Approval for Operation "Overlord" was one thing, but even then the Allies could not agree on strategy. In the run-up to the invasion there were heated disagreements, and at one time Eisenhower actually threatened to abandon his post. Most of the arguments were concerned with pre-invasion plans. Secrecy was of paramount importance, a fact that neither the British nor the Americans disputed. To this end, elaborate plans were implemented to ensure that the Germans were put off the scent. The British and Americans did disagree, however, on the best methods of undermining the German military machine prior to invasion. Eisenhower was certain that the only way to prevent German reinforcements from rallying to the coast the moment invasion occurred was to destroy the French communications network. A plan was contrived that would involve the intensive bombing of all French railway lines. Bomber commanders on both the British and American sides disapproved of the plan, stating that it was better to continue bombing raids on German oil supplies. Furthermore, they flatly refused to allow Leigh-Mallory (the RAF Air Chief Marshal) to take control of the heavy bombers.

Following much discussion, the bomber commanders were brought into line and it was agreed that the bombing of French railways would take place alongside a continued series of strikes against German oil supplies. Churchill was extremely hostile to the proposed assaults on the railway system. He argued that over 100,000 Frenchmen would be killed if such a plan were adopted. Eventually, Churchill was pacified by Eisenhower, and the pre-invasion bombing began. Certainly, Frenchmen were killed, but their casualties numbered 10,000 rather than 100,000, and the Free French General Koenig had been fatalistic about the campaign.

The most successful pre-invasion bombing campaign, however, was the one led by Leigh-Mallory. In just twenty-one days the tactical bombers under his command destroyed seventy-four tunnels and bridges with amazing accuracy. The successful destruction of these targets made it virtually impossible for the Germans to rally troops quickly. In addition, the heavy bombers had managed to inflict substantial damage on the German Luftwaffe. This effectively ensured that the British and American air forces would have air supremacy throughout the European invasion.

Nevertheless, the core of Operation "Overlord" relied fundamentally on the Navy. The naval operation designed to support "Overlord" was code-named "Neptune" and was commanded by Admiral Sir Bertram Ramsay. Clearly, the regular supply of troops, equipment, ammunition, materials, food and medicine all depended on the ability of British and American shipping to deliver. There were two major problems confronting the Navy. Firstly, the naval personnel needed to judge the best time for the invasion, given tides and weather. Secondly, they needed to find a safe anchorage for ships, since the proposed invasion was to take place on the Normandy coast. The first problem was resolved with relative ease; the second was more difficult. In the end, the Allies relied on the new "artificial harbour" system, devised by Commodore Hughes-Hallet. They simply transported the artificial harbours across the Channel and protected them with breakwaters.

In the event, bad weather almost prevented the Normandy invasion, originally planned for 5 June 1944. The Allies eventually landed on 6 June. Overall, the operation went well, largely because of the element of surprise. The British and Canadians came ashore at beaches code-named "Gold", "Juno" and "Sword", while the Americans landed at "Utah" and "Omaha". The British were initially more successful than the

Americans because they had the strong naval support. At "Utah", the Americans landed a mile off target and it took them until nightfall to establish a reasonable beachhead. At "Omaha" beach the story was quite different. The troops initially lacked adequate naval support, and rough seas had consumed many of their tanks and landing vessels. German troops at "Omaha" had recently been strengthened with a fresh contingent and the Americans were forced to attempt a desperate climb up into the cliffs. But many officers were killed almost as soon as they had hit the beach and overall losses were severe. Eventually, as the weather improved slightly, naval and aerial gunfire was able to provide better support and the troops managed to establish a small bridgehead by nightfall. But because they had been unable to counter German resistance successfully, they were unable to communicate with their fellow Americans at "Utah".

By the evening of D-Day the Allied grip on Normandy was tenuous, the sections had not connected in the manner that had been anticipated by the Allied command beforehand, and the Germans were beginning to gather strength. During the following two days, the Allies poured men and equipment into the beachheads along the coast and fighting began in earnest. By 9 June links were established between "Omaha" beach and the British beaches. The following day, Carentan was captured and a connection was made with "Utah". British and Canadian forces made their way towards Caen. But, as the frontline consolidated, bad weather interrupted events. On 19 June severe gales hit the

English Channel and ships were unable to deliver essential supplies to the troops. Without these supplies the Allies could not begin their planned attacks and progress ground to a virtual standstill.

Casualties during the initial invasion period had been heavy. Wounds were horrific, but were treated as soon as possible, with many of the early casualties simply evacuated back to England out of harm's way. As Nurse Collingwood remembered:

When D-Day started we had three tables in the theatre, three theatres working and after that, about the second and third days, they were coming in thick and fast. They flew them from the battlefields in France over to Epsom Downs and brought them straight in, so we often got patients that had only been wounded two or three hours, still with black faces. We worked for six weeks, I think, solidly from 6a.m. 'til midnight without any time off or anything, because there were instruments to scrub and sterilise, and gowns to sterilise, dressing drums to be packed. We didn't have the sterile packs that they have in hospital now. You had to make your own dressings and sterilise them. I remember that as one of the most enjoyable times of my life quite frankly, because we were so busy but it was so rewarding. I think it was about six weeks and then we were all given a week off because we hadn't had any time off and we were absolutely exhausted. We were all very young and we were able to work those long hours.

Not all the staff back in Britain were quite so happy about the evacuation of D-Day casualties. In a letter dated 26 June 1944, Sgd James Anderson wrote:

My dear Brigadier,

I am writing to confirm our conversation about the serious condition of several patients who arrived at Alverstoke E.M.S. hospital in convoys last Friday morning and night and append to several specific cases.

I feel that the medical officers who are evacuating cases from hospitals on the other side do not realise that the patients may be on board landing craft for two or even three days before they reach a hospital on this side and during these two or three days the patient's condition may deteriorate considerably. For example two cases had gas gangrene by the time that we got them. Again Plaster of Paris covers a multitude of sins and when this is applied the notes should describe the severity of the patient's injuries accurately. When a case comes to hospital near a beach, if it is in POP that doctor may easily look at this plaster — see that it is alright — ask if it is comfortable and then pass it on. Two of the patients should really have been held by the hospital on the beach. Almost without exception the medical attention that the patients have had has been beyond reproach but I note one exception below.

This patient had a terrible wound of the left buttock and thigh. Two thirds of the circumference of the limb including the femur was just not there. The early operation note stated that debridement of the wound had been carried out, a Tobruk plaster had been applied over a Thomas Splint and then he had been sent on his way. In the first place his leg should have been amputated if not at the FSU certainly in the General Hospital but the 3118 gave the hospital no idea of the severity of the wound.

I don't wish to be highly critical and the forward medical officers and surgeons have really done a splendid job. I merely wish to warn you that in their anxiety to keep beds available for fresh cases there is a danger that cases are being evacuated whilst they are still unfit for the arduous journey that lies ahead of them. I feel that it is possible that the officers who evacuate them may not realise that it takes so long for them to get to hospitals in England.

Although some of the wounded were evacuated from the battlefields by ship, and their journey was extremely drawn out and difficult, many were also airlifted back to England. The first batch of casualties were flown back to England to the tune of 400 a day. In all, over 50,000 troops were flown back, and this was no easy task, as the *British Journal of Nursing* proclaimed:

Fifty thousand casualties have been flown home by the RAF without one mishap, though more than 4,000 sorties, representing 1,500,000 miles of flying, have been made by Transport Command. The 50,000th was among the wounded troops to arrive in time to spend Christmas Day in an English hospital. As the volunteer stretcher-bearer airmen, giving up their leisure, carried out the lying cases, a medical orderly stopped ticking them off on a register and, approaching a soldier with head injuries, said "the 50,000th".

Furthermore, despite the reservations that were voiced by medical personnel in England with regard to the appalling state of some of these casualties, the message from the consultant surgeon in Normandy was reassuring:

First impressions on arrival here are that surgical restraint is being exercised and the technique and results appear good. Abdominal wounds less than 3% anaerobic infection appears prevalent. Penicillin being used freely; impressions favourable. There has been no shortage of fresh blood. Later, on 20 June 1944, the Director of Medical Services Army Group visited Normandy. A medical area had been established round Bayeux and marked off with Red Cross signs. The Director was impressed with the way in which the wounded were being dealt with. The weather was extremely bad while he was there; rain and high wind hampering tent pitching and offloading.

In many respects, the military medical planning could not be easily explained. Specialised civilian orthopaedic surgeons had been flown over to Normandy to give 'on the spot' care to invasion casualties. Then, just as the time came to administer this care they were told to exercise surgical restraint. It was not surprising, therefore, that the War Office was subsequently bombarded with complaints from the orthopaedic surgeons who had remained in England. These surgeons correctly pointed out that the lives of many casualties had been unnecessarily endangered because they had been forced to wait for operations that should have taken place in Normandy.

To some extent, the military had been caught out by the large numbers of D-Day casualties, but the speed with which some of these severely wounded men were dispatched to England amounted to sheer negligence.

The nurses assigned to the medical back-up units in France worked as far forward as possible, alongside the fighting forces. But how quickly each medical unit could become operational largely depended on the preparation work that had begun in England. "Every single bit of equipment had to be greased against rust, wrapped in oiled paper, stencilled with a code number, so that it could all be unpacked without any delay on the other side, wherever that was. In the end, when we put up our 75th British General Hospital in Normandy, we were operational within 48 hours, taking enormous numbers of casualties from Caen."

Just about all the military hospitals were operational within 48 hours, though nurses were often hard-pressed to complete the unpacking process before casualties arrived.

Each of us was detailed to a different part. For instance I was detailed to help unpack resuscitation. So it was then that the careful packing in England came about. You knew that crates belonging to resuscitation were labelled in a certain way. Crates were delivered and you got cracking immediately with claw hammers. Out came the nails and then out came the sacks and then out came the little bundles of oiled instruments. Orderlies came up and put up trestles for stretchers. The boards had to have these collapsible beds fitted out. And then it was all hands to the pump to make up the beds because it was operational in 48 hours.

In fact, our first casualties started coming in from Caen and we hadn't yet found the morphia. We were still diving into the bottom of a packing case to try and find the morphia. We found it pretty soon because it was pretty necessary, but that's how quickly things happened. It was mostly improvisation inside the tents. We had a trestle as a sort of instruments table, to put out the tray which would hold the sterilised syringes, and a small steriliser that was worked by spirit. Behind this we stacked the compo boxes, as we called them. They were wooden boxes that this compressed tea came in. We stacked them and they acted as shelves for various medicaments, and aspirins, and indigestion mixtures and plaster and bandages. We used to have a dustbin for splints, a big blood box somewhere handy, and there would be one or two drip stands handy.

Yet again nurses were in the frontline, and many were wounded or killed administering care. Nearly all agreed, however, that casualty clearing stations were usually bombed accidentally rather than intentionally by the enemy. As one nurse recalled:

I moved to a field dressing station which was obviously very noisy as it must have been very near the front, I just remember terrible wounds — we could only give very limited first aid. I don't know how many patients we had — it was quite a small tent and the patients were on the floor, on stretchers. Wherever there was a space there was a stretcher. There were RAMC orderlies who treated the patients on the spot as they were wounded and then they were carried back by stretcher bearers. At each stage the patient had a label stating roughly what his wounds were and what treatment had been given. Sometimes, because perhaps a casualty clearing station was rather near an important feature, it would come into the line of fire quite accidentally. It would not intentionally be attacked by the Germans.

But in Bayeux I think it was, 32 CCS set up near what was known as the Jerusalem crossroads in Bayeux, an airstrip was being put down there and the Germans got to know about it. So they bombed and bombed it and of course the CCS suffered and eventually had to move. One of the sisters was very badly injured, and another was wounded but not too badly. They had to move but they couldn't move the abdominals. An abdominal has to wait eight days before they can be moved, so the abdominals had to be left behind with a changing team of about three orderlies and one sister. In the meantime they put up lots of sandbags to try and make the casualty clearing tent a little more safe but, on occasions like that, they could catch it quite nasty.

Another nurse recalled that there was more concern for her virtue than for any potential injury from bombs: "We were only four sisters there amongst an awful lot of different groups. There were searchlights, artillery, pioneers and medical. The Colonel was terribly worried that our virtue was going to be attacked and so this enormous notice was put up, 'Sisters Quarters — Keep Out'. So the next day as we passed the engineers tent there was a great big notice saying: 'Brothers Quarters — Come In!'"

The most difficult problem to confront nurses at this stage in the war, however, was not the prospect of threatened virtue or enemy bombs, but actually having to nurse the enemy itself. There had been occasions earlier in the war when nurses had found themselves administering care to the enemy, but not in such great numbers. The German propaganda machine had filled the minds of German soldiers with all kinds of false rumours. Consequently, all of them feared medical treatment at the hands of the British and American medical teams.

The very first patient on D-Day was a German officer — I can't remember his rank — an army officer who had shrapnel in his buttocks, and he demanded to be taken to German occupied England. On being told that no part of England was occupied — it took a lot to convince him of this — he became very frantic with fright because he had been told that English doctors operated on prisoners of war without anaesthetic. It took five of us to hold him down to give him an anaesthetic.

These fears, of course, were unfounded and German prisoners of war received exactly the same medical treatment as everyone else, despite the fact that many of them, particularly the SS officers, did not want to live. "They didn't want to survive. Some of them pulled out their intravenous tubes when they were having a blood transfusion. They just wanted to die for the Führer and they jolly well did."

Most of the British medical personnel recognised, nonetheless, that German soldiers had been affected by the war and, particularly, the indoctrination process that accompanied Nazism. Most of the SS officers deliberately defecated on the floors, and British nurses and orderlies were forced to clean up their excrement on a daily basis.

Among them we had a few SS walking wounded and we hadn't enough people to guard them. They used to walk around and blow their tops. They were very arrogant. When we were nursing, and had bed, stretcher, bed, stretcher and we had this reception room. The place had been a little school. In the hall we had stretchers galore. You could hardly put your feet in between. We were luckily wearing our battledress kit and the Germans either did this to insult us or, I don't know. They used to mess on the floor and we had to put our gaiters on so that we didn't get the bottom of our trousers filthy. They were all in a very queer mental state. They wouldn't take food. They were told we were fattening them up to kill them.

It was also clear from a number of German soldiers captured that recruits were taken in to the German Army at a very young age, and that some were lying wounded for several days before being taken prisoner and receiving treatment: "They had been wounded a long time. They were very young boys. They were seventeen and eighteen and on their notes they had two years' service, some of them. They had the most ghastly wounds. This was where you could tell that the German medical treatment wasn't good. Amputations — limbs had just been chopped off. Suppurating wounds, necrosed bones [dead bone] and they looked terrible."

In all, 265,000 Germans were killed or wounded, and 350,000 were captured as prisoners of war during the bid to free France from German occupation. It had been an uphill struggle for the Allies and, frequently thwarted by bad weather and lack of supplies, progress had been slower than anticipated. At times relationships between the Allied commanders were still strained. Eisenhower was frustrated at the length of time taken by the British and Canadian forces to break out from frontline positions, whereas, in many respects, Montgomery had a firmer grasp on events as they were happening on the ground, and was naturally cautious as a consequence. The inability to capture Caen during the first stages of the invasion was viewed as a distinct British failure, when in fact Caen was heavily defended and Germans had been instructed to fight to the death rather than give up any territory. A war of attrition developed, which was largely dictated by the German defence. Furthermore, some of the geographical areas were not particularly suited to mobile warfare, and considerable adjustments had to be made to tanks before speedier progress could be achieved.

The battle for Caen began on 7 July. As a prelude to the Allied offensive, bombers subjected the town to blanket bombing raids. The next day, as the British reached the perimeters of the town, they found that many of the streets were blocked by rubble. The Germans had fled from the centre of the town and had "dug in" south of Caen. A German defensive line some 10 miles long had been established and, since they had ruined many of the bridges, the Allies were unable to follow them. Montgomery's renewed offensive on Caen began on 18 July, and yet again Allied bombers subjected the town to mass bombing. The first line of the German defence crumbled with relative ease, but the situation worsened as fighting developed in the villages alongside the Bourguebus Ridge. Over a period of two days, both sides sustained heavy losses but, although bad weather again prevented the capture of the ridge at Caen, all other goals were completed. The Germans were worn out and depleted. Nevertheless, Eisenhower was still not satisfied with progress. He berated both Montgomery and the American commander Bradley for their lack of energy, despite the fact that the former had been hampered by bad weather and the latter had been waiting for more ammunition supplies before he could stage any real offensives.

Eventually, on 25 July, Operation "Cobra" was launched. The operation planned to focus tank and aircraft forces on the point of weakness in the German line. Bradley's forces were strengthened and made ready for a final showdown. The American armoured tanks made substantial progress within the first few days of Operation "Cobra". Each forward unit was supported by fighter bombers, and German resistance was rapidly overcome. Following a period of sustained bombing, many of the Germans realised that the battle to retain territory was futile, and they surrendered. Bradley maintained the momentum and ordered his troops to continue to push forwards. Then, on 1 August, General George Patton entered the fray. Within three days Patton had seized nearly all of Brittany and had turned his attentions towards Paris. Rearguard actions by the Germans were rendered impotent in the face of Allied forces.

On 15 August the Allies landed in the south of France having consolidated their position in the north. With Free French support they urged forwards to connect with the American assault on Paris. There was little German resistance along the way. Many of the Germans were now running away at the sight of Allied forces. Paris was liberated on 25 August — to much celebration. Following this, on 4 September British troops arrived in Antwerp. Montgomery and the combined Allied forces recaptured the port but, in his enthusiasm to push towards Germany, Montgomery failed to clear the seaward entrance, hence rendering the port useless to the Allies. Since it had been intended to use Antwerp as a primary supply route in the drive towards Germany, the failure to gain sea access significantly delayed the supply of Allied troops and prompted an expensive and lengthy clearing operation. Thus Antwerp became the focal point of fighting throughout the autumn of 1944, giving the Germans plenty of time to regroup and plan substantial counter-offensives.

Meanwhile, the Allies had also launched Operation "Market Garden", which began on 17 September. In a combined air and land assault, the Allies intended to cross the Rivers Waal, Maas and Neder Rijn to support the British Second Army, which was advancing towards northern Germany. The British offensive strike took place at Arnhem but was quickly trapped by a German counter-offensive. The British airborne division, along with the Polish parachute brigade, held its position at Arnhem until the survivors managed to cross the Rhine on 25 September. Hasty planning and bad management had contributed to the British failure at Arnhem and it was a salutary lesson. Clearly, the Germans had strengthened their resistance. Nevertheless, the Allies were still well forward by the winter months of 1944, and although the strong German resistance encountered by Montgomery in the Netherlands also hampered Patton at Lorraine, some Allied forces were already in Germany.

Montgomery took time out to visit the injured.

I was with the maxillor-facial unit attached to the number 8 hospital in Brussels and, because I was a separate little unit, I didn't quite come under the rules of the host unit. So I was more or less allowed to go my own way, and I had an awful lot of dressings to do and I was the only one to do it. So while the rest of the hospital was polishing, and all this spit and polish was going on for Monty's visit, I was just getting on with my dressings. When he came, everybody was standing to attention except me.

I had my mask on and I was doing a dressing. He made a beeline for me and said, "I don't want to hold you up sister." He shook my hand and I shall always remember him. He had a grip like iron, and the piercing quality of his blue eyes was quite something — straight through. I really think he agreed with me in that this was not a priority, not the visiting brass hat. I felt that he thought I had made the right decision about that.

Montgomery was one of the officers who had fully supported the move to have nursing sisters working at the frontline alongside the fighting forces. This frontline policy, he argued, was good for the morale of the troops.

For their part, the injured troops would always try to instil some humour into the everyday life of the wards. Sometimes their humour backfired:

> I remember on one occasion going round and taking their temperatures. We had to do a lot at a time because we were very busy. I had six in a ward and I shot out to the next ward. When I came back of course, they had put their thermometers under the hot water tap so they had all shot up. This broke the thermometers and I said, "You'll have to find the mercury for me because I can't have them replaced until you do." When I went back about an hour later they said, "We can't find the mercury sister." I said, "Oh, it's alright I didn't want it." They nearly lynched me!

Despite the Allied advance, the Germans had still not surrendered and had no intention of doing so while they had at least some fight left. But by the end of December 1944, they were under attack from both sides. The Russians in the east marched towards the German heartland, and the American, British and French Armies, following their breakout at St-Lo, had advanced as far as the frontiers of the Reich. The Allied air raids on Germany were imposing and debilitating. Short of manpower, and with diminishing levels of industrial production, Germany was in the process of being reduced to rubble. The German military machine, nonetheless, still had some might, and Hitler planned a massive counter-offensive through the Ardennes in an attempt to regain the initiative on his western flank. His primary aim was to thrust towards Antwerp and split the British and American forces, thereby stabilising his western front. Some of the German High Commanders believed that it was tactically safer merely to restore the western wall, but in the event they were overruled.

The last and major German counter-offensive, which later became known as the "Battle of the Bulge" (because of the bulge that was created in the American lines), began on 16 December 1944 and took the Allies completely by surprise. Initially, the American forces sustained severe losses and fell back, but they managed to hold fast and the Germans were unable to break through. Eisenhower instructed Patton to attack the German left flank, and promptly placed the American units cut off by communication disruptions under the command of Montgomery. Thus a coordinated response was maintained, and the Battle of the Bulge became the largest land battle fought by the Americans during the whole of the Second World War. Some of the American defensive positions were only maintained because of the involvement of non-combatant personnel such as cooks, orderlies and clerks.

The Germans had interrupted communications at Meuse by implementing a duplicitous plan code-named Operation "Grief", whereby a number of Germans, dressed as American soldiers and equipped with stolen Jeeps, had captured bridges and disrupted the communication networks. This deception was uncovered eventually, but there is no doubt that the confusion did slow down Allied progress. Spot checks were introduced to ascertain the identity of personnel. To prove he was not a German spy, each American soldier had to recall the name of Betty Grable's husband or the strategic playing positions adopted by famous players in American football teams. This system worked well for the Americans (though the process of checking slowed the relief forces moving up from the rear), but it was hopeless for the British, who had no idea about American football and were totally unconcerned about Betty Grable's marital status! Montgomery ended up having to carry an American identity card, and some ludicrous situations developed. Some British officers were imprisoned by the Americans for hours, simply because they did not know all the answers to American spot-check interrogations.

Despite the confusion, a combination of swift and substantial Allied reinforcements and isolated bouts of heroism halted the German advance. The Germans were unable to make further advances at any rate because they were short of fuel. Difficult terrain and bad weather also impeded their progress. Once the weather improved in late December, the Allies were able to bring fighter planes to bear on the situation. Consequently, by the beginning of January 1945, the Germans were in retreat and the "bulge" was rapidly diminishing in size. The Germans had lost 100,000 men and 1,000 planes, along with numerous items of equipment. The subsequent Rhineland battles of February and March 1945 inflicted major defeats on Germany. Over 300,000 Germans were killed in those two months alone. The disarray and sense of defeatism was clear among the remaining German units.

An Allied victory in Europe was now assured, and on 30 April 1945 Hitler committed suicide, blaming all and sundry for the German defeat. Rommel had already committed suicide the previous autumn. On 2 May German forces in Italy surrendered and by 8 May the German High Command had capitulated. The actual signing of the surrender took place at 2a.m. on 7 May, and by midnight of the same day Britain was celebrating like never before. Public holidays were granted for 8 and 9 May; street parties were in full swing up and down the country; and Britain's naval vessels sounded a siren of salute in honour of the long-awaited victory.

With the onset of peace in Europe, Churchill was removed from power in the 1945 general election and his government replaced by a Labour government. The nursing press expressed its regret at his replacement, and their thanks for his service to the country:

Thousands of registered nurses with the deepest sense of gratitude and loyal devotion, who realise that they owe to Mr Winston Spencer Churchill, late Premier and Minister of Defence, the great victory of the war in Europe, the continued existence of Great Britain and the Empire, and indeed the stability of the world, wish to convey to him their love and loyalty. No words can express their admiration of, and devotion to, the man of genius to whom the whole world owes its hope of human life worthy of existence. It is the proud privilege of the editor of this journal to place on record this quite inadequate expression of gratitude to the pilot who weathered the storm.

Churchill had been relieved of power primarily because he had not offered the country anything new for the postwar years, whereas the Labour government planned to establish a National Health Service (NHS) and a comprehensive welfare state. However, despite these plans, wartime austerity and rationing was to continue for some years. Contrary to popular belief, nurses were not particularly in favour of the idea of an NHS. Most nurses were traditionalists and favoured the continuation of the voluntary hospital system. They were even less enamoured with the Labour chancellor Hugh Dalton, particularly when he proposed that nurses needed to work harder to make up for the existing staff shortages. To add insult to injury, Dalton suggested that nurses should no longer be considered a priority in terms of obtaining extra food rations to cope with their strenuous work.

The nursing press was furious and dedicated a whole page to the subject. The article was deeply sarcastic:

A cut in our meagre rations is threatened. Nurses have no priority and thus they will have to carry out their arduous tasks on a less intake of energy and body-building materials. This hardship will not affect older nurses so seriously as it will affect the younger ones. Now Mr Dalton's blessing, benevolent as it is, and most unexpected and staggering, will not supply the necessary calories required by nurses to carry out their daily tasks. Can he supply them with anything likely to appease hunger pangs more efficaciously than by his non-episcopalian blessing?

Clothing coupons are to be in "short supply" over a longer period. Perhaps that won't affect nurses quite so badly, because they wear uniform for a long period of their earthly lives, which is coupon free. Still, their stockings wear out so quickly and their shoes get holes in them with such startling rapidity that one wonders if it might not be a good idea to copy the mediaeval Franciscans or Discalced Monks, and go barefooted or else press for exciting sandals made of nice soft leather, which leave bare toes and heels comfortably free!

"Ah", thinks one bright young thing, "I will go abroad for holidays and stock up my wardrobe and have a jolly good feed and then return home ready for anything!" Unfortunately for her Mr Hugh Dalton thought first, and this time — without his blessing — he arranged that only a small amount of petty cash should accompany hungry British travellers abroad looking for "extras". So the bright young thing must think again.

Once again our wily chancellor has the answer to it. Nurses like everyone else must WORK! Yes — really work! Up to now nurses haven't worked at all, they've only THOUGHT they did. So now, what about taking a plot of ground in one's off-duty time and growing one's own tomatoes, spinach, asparagus, grapes, and other luxuries, one has grown accustomed to having lately. On one's day off, why not "volunteer" to work in a mill or factory, or even down a coal mine? Perhaps nurses sleep too long? Very well, cut down on sleep and volunteer for part-time night work in the nearest cottage hospital or relieve the "hard-pressed" char woman and clean the corridors and front steps. There is always MORE WORK to be done if one looks hard enough for it.

You'll probably earn more money by undertaking these little extra jobs — perhaps you won't be quite sure what to do with it. Leave it to Mr Dalton — God bless him — he'll tell you what to do! After deducting his share of income tax, you may then buy War Savings or National Savings Certificates! Then, when you get older and the zest for living is departing and you no longer crave silk undies, nylons, creams and chocolates and glamorous holidays, you will have plenty of money to buy all you require for your old age. Now isn't Mr Dalton a pet to think all this out so nicely for us?

So now we realise that for the great boon of being born and bred British, we must pay for the privilege. We've won the war, we've weathered the bombs and blast and now we've to crack and crush the crisis. Is this too much for British nurses to endure? No — no — a thousand times no — but let it be the last crisis, please! Some day — in the not too distant future — give us our perfumes and fine soaps, our stockings and shoes, our bright lights at night. Give us more nurses to share our burdens, and send us good cooks and chars without pains, and then, Mr Dalton, our work will be a pleasure and you won't have to plead with us to work or want. We'll work.

Civilian registered nurses were still smarting from the 1943 Nurses Act, which had allowed "faith healers" to call themselves "nurse", and it was not surprising that they reacted to measures that would threaten their priority claim for food rations. As far as they were concerned, the measures represented yet another way of undermining their profession. Many nurses believed that their contribution to the war effort had not been adequately recognised and that their whole profession was undervalued within British society. The war in Europe had been won but for civilian nurses the battle for status had been lost.

CHAPTER
SEVEN

Tenko

By 1945 the war was over in Europe, but the fighting continued in the Far East. Nurses who had been captured and imprisoned by the Japanese knew nothing of the victory in Europe. As Dame Margot Turner recalled, "We didn't have a radio. So sometimes one of the guards might give us some information but nothing much. We just lived on rumours. We didn't really know what was happening. We didn't know the war had ended, until I suppose, it must have been a long time afterwards." The imprisoned nurses also discovered that their officer status gave them no protection against Japanese brutality. Japanese soldiers simply refused to believe that any women in the British armed forces could even aspire to such a rank. Thus the story of the nurses held captive by the Japanese stands as the most harrowing of all the nurses who served during the war.

In 1942 Nurse Betty Blanc-Smith wrote to her mother from Singapore:

New Year's Day! and I must simply write you a long letter to make up for the lapse of time since my last effort. I sent you a cable the day after the war started out here as I knew you would be worried. They assured me at the cable office that it would reach you by Christmas and I do hope that it did so. Goodness knows when you will get this, but I hope it will be before next year! Now there is no "clipper" service, news will be long in reaching you but don't worry about me — whatever may happen to me cannot but be for the best, and so far I seem to have been so well cared for that I see no reason why protection should suddenly cease, and whatever I go through is all experience and proves one's strength of character and fundamental beliefs. I have no fear for myself and at the present look on life as a great adventure with the unexpected round every corner. I have often felt that this part of the world must be brought into line with the rest of nations, because its God is money. Many people finding themselves now left with nothing are learning life's true values, perhaps for the first time. I think I already know them up to a point, but that has yet to be proved and there is so much to learn.

To hold life so cheaply and all one's worldly possessions of no account takes some doing, but it is the lesson many have to learn until experience has taught us it is impossible to forecast reactions. Waiting for the baptism of fire doesn't worry me much except for the usual empty feeling at the sound of planes and guns. One sister here has been through France, the Middle East and Greece with amazing experiences and I want to do likewise. At last my existence here seems about to be justified and the year of "fun and games" preceding this was just the prelude and will be something to be remembered with a tolerant smile.

On 17 April 1942 Betty's parents received a letter from the War Office stating that their daughter was posted as missing, presumed to have been captured or killed by the Japanese during the fall of Singapore on 15 February 1942. The Japanese had swept through European colonial outposts at an alarming rate. Hong Kong, Manila and much of Malaya was in Japanese hands by the end of January 1942. The following is the testimony of Mrs E.A. Fidoe, a state registered nurse who was working at St Stephen's College, Hong Kong, at the time of the Japanese invasion in December 1941:

There was sniping and shelling going on all day long. The patients were all in the main hall and the staff were — the majority of them — gathered outside. There was shelling all night. About quarter to seven — it was difficult to know the time, it was dark in the morning — we suddenly heard shots and cries. I thought at first that one of our own men had gone mad as there were one or two of them who had shell shock. I then realized that bayonets were poking through the blanket curtains covering the doors. The Japanese had come into the small hall and staircase up on the other side. They ran up the staircase and got amongst us and seemed to be more concerned in taking all our jewellery. The first thing I knew was that a man had his arms up my sleeve and had taken my jewellery. They then burst onto the railings on the other side and started shooting down into the main hall.

There was a small room leading off the hall and they bundled us into that small room and locked us up. There were quite a number of patients and several dead bodies lying in pools of blood. I think there were about 30 of us in that room, patients and nurses. After we had been there for about two hours, the Japanese opened the door and ordered us all out and to go upstairs. This wounded soldier had crawled out of the main hall with his splint hanging off and had dragged himself into that room. He was also ordered upstairs with us. He could not walk and I had to put my arm on his elbow and help him. A Japanese shouted at me and beat me up. He beat my arm with the butt end of a rifle.

On the first floor we were all divided up and forced into little rooms. All day long Japanese soldiers came in and out of the room. They stood staring at us and searched us for any valuables we might have and we heard screams from various parts of the building. It would be difficult to describe where the screaming was coming from. There was a young Canadian soldier in the room with me. He had a wound in his arm and had been bayoneted again. We asked for bandages but they refused to give them to us.

At about that time [5 o'clock on Christmas Day 1941] two Japanese soldiers came along and made us, the nurses, stand up. They looked us up and down for half an hour and took away one and she did not come back. After a while they came back and beckoned to the two of us left and made us follow them along the corridor into a small room which I learned was one of the master's studies and left us there. The small study we were shown into had some Chinese women there when we got there. I think there were five.

These Chinese women, two of them were crying and there was a small bathroom out of the room and Japanese soldiers came and took them one after the other into the bathroom. They tried to resist but could not. This lasted about an hour. There were two mattresses on the floor. We thought we were going to be left there for the night to rest. A little afterwards a Japanese soldier came into the room and asked for one of us to go and bandage the wounded soldiers. One would not go without the other and Miss Gordon, Nursing Sister, myself and two VADs insisted on going together. We followed these soldiers along the corridor and they took us into a small room with mattresses on the floor. They pushed us down on the floor and proceeded to rape us too.

I would say that while the soldiers were in there with us, another was standing with fixed bayonet outside the door, and suddenly the door was thrown open and the soldier beckoned to the others and they hurried us away along the corridor. They took us back to the room we had left formerly. There were no Chinese women there any more. They had all gone. There were just four of us there and we shut the door. The mattresses had also been taken away. It was quite empty. We stayed in that room all night being visited by Japanese soldiers until we were so distraught we would not open the door any more.

We were raped from time to time. Every time a soldier left — the door had a slip lock — we locked it. We were so upset we just did not care what happened and would not open the door. They thought there was some of their own kind in there, so they left us alone for two hours. There was a window looking out of the room where we stood and we watched the Japanese taking out mattresses, blankets and bodies and putting them on lorries and covering them up with blankets. I could not see who they were.

I saw them taking tables and chairs from the college and building up a huge mound which they set fire to. I saw them putting the dead bodies on the fire. Sometime after daybreak we heard footsteps and then the dental surgeon, Col McCurdie, knocked at the door together with a Japanese officer and some Japanese soldiers. Col McCurdie told us two of our own wounded were downstairs and he wanted us to go down and attend to them. He was only a dental surgeon. He was not a doctor. We went down and found two Canadian soldiers with small injuries in their feet and wrists. They had walked to the hospital over the hills, not knowing we had surrendered.

We rendered first aid to the two Canadian soldiers and then we were told to go back upstairs and we could attend to our wounded. When we got back up there we found all the rooms had been opened up and everyone was in the process of cleaning the place. There were lots of feathers about. We went down on our hands and knees and cleaned the place until dark. We found among the feathers some dead bodies. We then got some first aid equipment which we got from the store room downstairs and we attended the wounded. We found in every case the splints had been taken off, the bandages had been cut and many of the men were bleeding rather badly and quite a few had bayonet wounds all over them.

This volunteer officer took us away about 5 o'clock. We had, with some medical orderlies, dressed most of their wounds before we left them. We then went up to the fort. I have overlooked one thing. When we were called upstairs to attend the wounded, the husband of one of the volunteer nurses came and asked me if I knew where his wife was. She had been the one taken out of my room.

The name was Begg. He asked if I knew where she was. I told him she had been taken away. He came back with a Japanese officer and went round to search for her. He then came back and asked me to go with the Japanese officer. We met the Canadian padre and together with an orderly went down to the gardens and the other side of the nullah. The Japanese would not let anybody cross except me. There was a blanket by some bushes. I lifted the blanket and saw three bodies of volunteer nurses. One was the body of Mrs Begg, the wife of the husband I spoke about, another Mrs Smith and the other Mrs Buxton. They were stripped, devoid of all clothing, except for a coat belonging to Mrs Smith which was thrown over the bodies. Mrs Begg had been shot. There was a definite wound in her head. I saw throat wounds on the other two. It looked as though they had clean cuts through them. I saw the Japanese collect these bodies and put them on the funeral pyre.

I went back to where Captain Barnett and the RAMC orderly were waiting. I went to pieces a little bit. The Japanese officer — he was very young — shook me. He said, "You lucky. Three minutes and you would have gone too. Hong Kong surrendered just in time." Those were his words.

The testimony of Mrs Fidoe was given at a war crimes trial and, sadly, her experience was not an isolated one. Similar atrocities occurred throughout the Japanese invasion. Miss Amy Williams was working at the Jockey Club relief hospital as matron on 25 December 1941:

Three Japanese came along with trees in their helmet and with bayonets and one had a hand grenade and one had a revolver as well as a bayonet. They told us to stand up. There were some lying on the floor. They went around us with a torch. He chose five girls and told them to go along with him.

During the afternoon, all the Chinese, bar two nurses and one doctor, disappeared. We had increased in staff by this time. When air raid shelters were bombed out, they sent the staff to us to house them. We had by this time 195 staff, chiefly of course, Chinese. During the afternoon when they realised what was happening, they disappeared. By evening time we had only two nurses and one doctor and they escaped during the night. Of the five they released two of those girls. They raped three only of that lot. Afterwards they came down again and took four more up. In all six Europeans were raped, two of them twice.

After these happenings it was quiet until the next day. Then about 12 o'clock one of the Japanese came in and took one of the girls, dragging her by the arm through the ward. An officer appeared at the far end of the ward and he dropped her quickly and she fell on the bed. That was the end of the rape.

The transcripts of the war crimes trials make for grim reading, especially in cases where nurses were mutilated as well as being raped. The above testimonies are all the more shocking because the attacks took place on Christmas Day and were directed against medical personnel who were all wearing Red Cross arm bands (these were ripped off by the invading Japanese forces), and patients who were already injured.

The British government was not particularly surprised by the surrender of Hong Kong but British propaganda had made much of the ability of Singapore to withstand a Japanese attack, though Churchill admitted privately that Singapore was not a substantial fortress. However, he also claimed that, in looking at the wider picture, Burma was of more importance than Singapore. Burma was situated on the land road to India, and was a vital reinforcement link to China. Both Roosevelt and Churchill believed that if Burma was lost the Chinese, instead of maintaining the fight against Japan, might consider forming a pact with the Japanese and thereby establish a major "Pan-Asiatic" force.

This fear was also shared by the Australians, who were extremely alarmed by the advancing Japanese and felt let down by the British who had not rushed in to reinforce the Australian position. Despite protestations to the contrary, it was clear that Churchill had put the war in the Far East on the back burner until the war in Europe had been settled. This policy damaged relationships between Britain and Australia, particularly since the latter had declared war against Germany on the same day as Britain and had offered every support in the way of troops and equipment. Churchill, however, had chosen to defend Britain first and foremost and place colonial interests second. Therefore, although Allied troops put up a steady fight against the Japanese, Singapore was effectively doomed.

The Japanese invasion of Singapore was barbaric to say the least. As Japanese soldiers entered the hospitals they machine-gunned patients while they were still in their beds. Some patients were killed as they lay on the tables in the operating theatres. Nurses who were unable to escape from their wards were raped, beaten and killed.

As many of the British and Indian troops as possible, along with some refugees, were evacuated by sea.

Nurse Woodcock, who was serving on a hospital ship at the time of Singapore's capitulation, wrote the following from the Indian command:

My posting came through for theatre duty on a hospital ship to bring casualties off the beachheads in the Far East. We were just outside Singapore when it was being surrendered. Hong Kong had been given over too by the time we arrived. The patients we took on board were all Indian and all suffered from some deficiency or other. They had suffered much hardship and privation, some could only be fed on milk and soup, they were so weak. To add much to their troubles we ran into a typhoon on the way back, and hit the coral reef off the Nicobar islands. An oil tank was pierced and the ship soon caught fire. How those patients eventually got ashore without one casualty is a miracle. Fortunately all the patients were dressed in white, and from the light of the burning ship, and with the aid of the few lifeboats and rafts that were serviceable all 900 got safely ashore.

Among the flood of troops and refugees who attempted to leave the island as soon as it was captured were some of the military and civilian nursing sisters. Phyllis Thoms remembered:

Bombs were dropping all round us and we expected to be hit at any moment. The civilians were sent south. As nursing sisters we naturally stayed on although we were civilian nursing sisters, but four days later the Army told us to go. So we put as many patients as we could into ambulances and trucks and things. Anyone who could walk was sent home. The majority we sent away. I always remember: there was one little baby whose mother had died and no relations had come to collect this new-born child. I was very worried about this because I felt I could not take a new-born baby away, and I offered the baby to one of the attendants, a cleaning woman, and she was quite happy to take this little baby. She promised she would give it a good home. It was a dear little baby, only a few days old. So I hope it had a happy life after that.

There was a complete stream of men, women and children, and vehicles of every description, many with mattresses tied to the roofs of their cars because they were dive bombing and shelling all the time, and people with rickshaws and bicycles. Movement was very slow. Everybody was going south trying to get away from the fighting which was coming further south daily.

The ship was called the *Mata Hari* which sounds rather exotic, but it was a small cargo ship which normally took nine passengers, but in the end there were over 350 people squeezed on the deck and down below. A Japanese vessel followed us during the third night going along, with searchlights on us from this Japanese vessel. Our captain said we only had one small gun, we had no power to resist these people. At daylight this Japanese vessel came very close to us; the Japanese captain and two other sailors came on board, all with swords, and as he came on the deck (and it was crowded with women and children) there was complete silence. They went and met our captain but we were told to stay put for the moment but in due course we were all to go ashore.

One of the girls who had not been married very long had, I suppose, grabbed a few things in not a very practical way but she did not want to leave a canteen of new cutlery behind. So she came on board with her canteen of cutlery. She knew she couldn't carry this ashore so she was handing out cutlery and I managed to get a good-sized teaspoon, and that teaspoon was the only piece of cutlery I had for the next three and a half years.

Although some women and children were taken prisoner from boats that managed to reach the shore, others suffered the horrors of near drowning. As Dame Margot Turner recalled of her second shipwreck experience:

We had a light flashed on us and then I think we were shelled. The ship went down in about five minutes with everybody on board. I again found myself in the water and, with another QA who I didn't know at the time was badly wounded, we managed to tie two small rafts together. There was just room for someone to sit on the raft and hold a baby. Gradually people drifted away, what with the sun and everything, and in the end I was left with one other lady — we were just sitting back to back. We had to paddle with our hands because we could see land but the currents were so queer there. At any rate she had this little bit of wood and it went and she went with it, and I was left alone. So I was there by myself for a day and a night, which was the fourth night I think. There were plenty of sharks around but of course they had got so much to eat. There were so many ships that had been sunk during that week. And then I saw a great ship coming. But of course it happened to be a Japanese ship and I, of course, was burnt black by the sun and I think they probably thought I was Malay. At any rate they picked me up. Someone came down with a rope and tied it round me, and hauled me over the top.

Dame Margot's ordeal was far from over. On board ship the numerous blisters she had acquired in the sun became infected and were lanced with a blunt knife. She had survived by eating seaweed and drinking rainwater she had managed to collect in the lid of a powder compact. Dame Margot was initially interned at Banka, a small island near Sumatra. Food rations were limited to two bowls of rice a day, which occasionally included a small amount of dried octopus:

Oh yes, we were always hungry. I had never eaten rice in my life until I landed up as a prisoner and was given my first bowl of rice. I just said to the person who gave it me that I didn't eat rice and they said I'd better because that was all I was going to get. On the whole it was rice in a little bowl with some rotten vegetables. Once we had a monkey which was very nice. It tasted like hare stew for 600 people. But then quite a few people didn't eat it so we had a bit more. Occasionally we might get a bit of fish. But I hate to see food wasted because I know what it is to be hungry. I always say if you are hungry you would eat anything. If you don't like a thing then you are not hungry. Otherwise you would eat it. The other thing that was a bit alarming to begin with, but didn't worry me unduly, was when I went to the washroom to have my daily dipper bath, a Japanese guard just stood and gazed at you, just to see what a white woman looked like in the nude. But it was much better not to worry about them and to feel cool with a wash.

We had one case where one of our orderlies was very badly slashed across the back of the neck and one of the Japanese realized it was he who had done it and said, "Aah" pointing to himself, and he produced a great bag of sugar for this man. They were your enemy one minute and your friend the next. After we were captured and our diet was so poor, gradually we stopped menstruating. After a few months everybody stopped having periods, which really was a good thing because nothing was ever supplied for us in that way, so really it was a mercy. People were so weak you see, they just couldn't do things. No energy, no strength, and just ill. A lot of them just gave up. They couldn't stand the future not knowing what might happen. Some heard that their husbands had died. This is what happened. The Japanese would perhaps tell them six months later, or would tell the husbands that their wives had died, which was a terrible thing. But not straightaway.

The treatment meted out to those incarcerated by the Japanese varied from one camp to another. Many women, including nurses, were undoubtedly treated very badly, raped, tortured and sometimes killed. Women took great pains to look unattractive so as not to warrant the attention of Japanese guards. Some women fought back when attacked and raped. They were brutally wounded as a result. Others were tortured by sadistic guards who insisted on giving them electric shock treatment while their bodies were wet and naked. It was not uncommon for a Japanese guard to come into the main compound of the camp each night, or even onto the prison hospital wards, and choose the woman he intended to rape. Since many women did not return the next morning all women prisoners lived in fear of being chosen.

Even if the women managed to escape the sexual and sadistic attentions of the guards they were still required to work under exhausting conditions with very little food.

186

We had to cut down trees to get firewood for the fire for cooking, carry the sacks of rice, carry the water. When we were let out we had to get water. And then we had to fill up the Japanese baths and water their gardens before they allowed us to bring any into the camp. We dug all the graves, buried all the dead — we had to do it quickly there. I think we made about three cemeteries, but I don't suppose they are there now. They would be overgrown. We were just coolies.

The guards used to tramp through with a torch each night, and they used to knock my shins with the butt end of their rifles. I never knew whether it was to keep me awake or to wake me up to cover my legs if there were mosquitoes. I never knew whether it was done viciously or otherwise. We were never physically manhandled, not then.

Whenever you saw a Japanese, no matter what rank, you had to bow and bow properly to them — low. We used to have tenko, a roll call every day, and stand at attention opposite our huts and, as we were counted (they counted us every day) we had to bow as they came by us. Most of the guards were very, I think, uneducated peasant-types, who couldn't count to more than ten. They would start off itchi nee, sansee, go and stop, and start again very often. If you didn't bow low enough you got your face slapped. One of the girls had a tooth knocked out one day because she felt, "Why should she, a British Army sister bow to a Japanese guard?" As long as you did what they said they didn't interfere with one unduly.

The girl who had her tooth knocked out because of her act of defiance was Dame Margot Turner. The "Tenkos" were always held in the heat of the day and many women collapsed as they waited to be counted by the roadside. For some of the time Dame Margot was able to use her nursing skills in captivity. A group of nurses were used to nurse Malays and Chinese in a native hospital. Then, without warning and with no explanation, Dame Margot and three other nurses were thrown into a jail at Palemburg. Other prisoners included thieves and murderers, who generally treated the nurses with respect and a degree of kindness. Several of the prisoners were beaten on a regular basis and many died as a result. When the nurses were finally released they were taken back to the camp, which had been relocated to a small swampy area, crawling with vermin and extremely cramped. The women tried to improve their lot by establishing choirs and language lessons. These were banned, however, when a new commandant was appointed to the camp in 1944. The frequency of "Tenkos" was increased, and women died in greater numbers from hard labour and starvation.

Army reserve nurse Brenda MacDuff kept a diary throughout her ordeal at a camp in Bankinang. The following extracts are just some of the entries she made in 1944 and 1945:

5 March 1944: The Japs have kept us very busy during the last three or four days, picking seeds out of cotton. It isn't really an unpleasant job, except that it makes one's fingers rather sore. A few weeks ago they brought some in and anyone who wanted to earn extra sugar picked it. Most of us refused because we were afraid the Japs might be going to use the seeds for war purposes. However, this time it was a rush order, we had no choice: everybody over 8 years had to do it, and quickly.

1 April 1944: We were handed over by the civilian Nipponese (we had to call them Nipponese, and certainly not the Japs) to the Army. Conditions seemed much the same, except we got a small meat ration once a week instead of every ten days. We discovered that the jail bed bugs had managed to make the long journey from Padang in people's mattresses. They liked the new conditions and multiplied exceedingly. We also have rats in the camp and Kutus (head lice).

13 June 1944: We heard a rumour that France had been invaded, starting on the 6th of June. Early in June an old lady, Mevrouw (Mrs) Teufenet died after a stroke. A few days after her death another old woman said that she had had a dream that Mevr Teufenet appeared to her, mad with anger because she had been sent to heaven without her false teeth, and declared that now there would be many more deaths in the camp on account of this. Last week there were four deaths, and the average is six per month, so the old lady will have plenty of listeners for her dreams in future, and we, incidently, will have to be more careful about false teeth!

8 August 1944: Rats are a menace here now — they eat everything they can put their teeth into and know no fear. We are dealing with them with large iron traps.

12 March 1945: 73 people who had been living in Padang, either working for Nippon or their husbands had been doing so, were brought into the camp. We took it as a good sign, that they should suddenly be interned after being more or less free for three years. It was said that there were another 200 to come in; we wondered where we would put them as nine of this lot had to be put in a wood shed.

2 April 1945: We had a most unpleasant experience last night. There was a very bad storm on — lightning, thunder and heavy rain. I was on night duty in a dysentery ward. One of the two rotten little Japanese oil lamps had blown out and it was very dark. Then suddenly there was a terrific clap of thunder and I saw sparks flying around. Then the screaming began. I ran out of the ward and saw the "attap" of the roof of the bathroom, a few yards away, on fire. It was put out within ten minutes, but whilst it lasted it was pretty frightening. I got all the patients up in case it spread. The fire and sparks were caused, they say, by a fireball. One of the Indonesian policemen on guard and holding a rifle at the time, collapsed and he died the following day.

11 April 1945: The men in the civilian camp have had a bad epidemic of dysentery. Every day one or two more die. If they have wives or relations in our camp they are sent for to attend the funeral. How dreadful for some of these women to have lived for three years without seeing their husbands and now when we hope it is near the end they are suddenly sent for to attend the funeral. Several young mothers with children died of tuberculosis. I remember two sad cases where the fathers were allowed to come in for a while and sit and talk to their children; in one case a girl and boy about 8 and 6, and another where there was a small boy about 5 and a baby born early in the internment days who might have been 2 and a half years old.

10 July 1945: Dr Lyon got a chance to talk to the camp Commandant. She hoped to be able to get some news out of him, but nothing doing, except that he told her that Mr Roosevelt was dead and added that Churchill was a fat old pig who would never die! The Commandant then went on to say that the war would last another 100 years.

16 July 1945: A rumour was going round the camp that 200 Japanese officers had committed "Hari Kari", and the locals outside the fence think the war will be over by the end of the month. During the last year or so a fair bit of smuggling has been going on at night: jewellery going out under the fence and food such as sugar and small sweet bananas (pisang mas) coming in. Not everybody can smuggle; I think one has to be in with the Indonesian guards. It is a dangerous job, but I have not heard of anyone being caught. I removed my engagement ring from nearly the bottom of a vaseline jar where, with Dr Lyons' permission, I had been allowed to hide it all this time. One of the women who did smuggle arranged to sell it for me through the fence. She got 500 guilders for it, and I gave her a quarter of that back for commission. These were not Dutch guilders, but Japanese "banana money" — only of use in the camp to buy smuggled sugar etc. Of course I gave some of it away and it meant that Marjory and I could now buy a few necessities from people in the camp. For instance Marjory, being small, was able to buy a pair of boy's shoes which he had grown out of. Later Marjory sold a signet ring (better not to let both rings go at once because there was always the risk that the buyer on the other side would not hand over the money).

We all wear wooden "trompas": shoes made of wood with a piece of canvas over the toes held on both sides by two nails. Our feet stick in the mud, with the result that the canvas breaks away — most annoying in the dark, on the frequent trips to the loos (a 200 yard sprint — a rice diet is not the best for an undisturbed night!).

We were a pretty unattractive lot by now. In fact I believe a visiting Japanese was heard to say that he had never seen such a lot of ugly women. And no wonder after so long on a very poor diet — no vitamin tablets in the camp of course. No dentist, not even any toothpaste, no perms, not even any decent soap or shampoo. We washed our hair in cold water, using the ration of one bar a month each of soap which, a Dutch woman told me, was the kind they would not have washed their clothes with in peacetime. Soap was very precious and to be guarded!

Rumours about the war were rife in the camp and it was difficult for the women to maintain their morale. Dame Margot Turner recalled that:

We didn't know the war in Europe was over. Various rumours used to filter through the camp, I think sometimes deliberately started by the Japanese. On one occasion they said, "Buckingham Palace has been bombed and all the royal family have been killed." But we wouldn't believe these things. Though we always felt that perhaps there was some truth in it, and of course years later we did hear what had happened. Then, one day, one of the guards said to one of the Dutch women that there had been a very big bomb somewhere but not in Sumatra, and that was all we knew.

The Allied decision to drop the atomic bomb was not taken lightly. It was considered to be the only way of forcing the Japanese to surrender. There had been several significant battles between the Allies and the Japanese following the fall of Singapore, of which the nurses were understandably unaware. The first decisive victory for the Allies came about during the naval Battle of Midway, which took place between 3 and 6 June 1942. Under the command of Yamamoto, a strategic plan was executed that involved dividing the combined fleet into eight task forces designed to stage a series of attacks on the atoll of the Midway. The Japanese aim was to coax Admiral Nimitz's fleet away from Pearl Harbor and force a confrontation at sea. However, Admiral Nimitz had prior knowledge of the forthcoming attack via the United States Army and Navy intelligence service, which was code-named "Magic". Armed with this knowledge, Admiral Nimitz was able to muster two task forces, under the command of Rear Admiral Fletcher, which were able to meet up at the northern point of the island and await the Japanese attack.

The remarkable American victory at Midway set the stage for the first American offensive at Guadalcanal. The Japanese had lost four fleet carriers and many experienced pilots at Midway and their defeat was keenly felt. More importantly for the Allies, the Japanese had lost the strategic advantage. The Japanese prime minister General Tojo appointed himself to the position of Chief of Staff in February 1944 in order to have total control over the Japanese war effort. However, the Japanese war effort had been steadily undermined from the Battle of Midway onwards, and Tojo was forced to resign in July 1944. The combination of Allied offensives, the American blockade of Japan (denying Japan the raw materials needed to make weapons), and the stepping up of bombing raids on mainland Japan in 1945 were all distinct signs of progress in the overall Allied war effort — much to the relief of the Australians, who had firmly believed that they were next on the list for a Japanese invasion. Once the American forces had captured Iwo Jima and Okinawa the Allied air raids were increased and coordinated with shelling from offshore warships. However, despite the grim outlook, the Japanese government flatly refused to accept the Allied terms of unconditional surrender.

Given that, to the Japanese, the question of surrender was a matter of honour versus dishonour, it was unlikely that an unconditional surrender would ever have been forthcoming. No Japanese official would take the decision to surrender for fear of being executed for dishonourable conduct. Thus, without the atomic bomb the war in the Far East might have dragged on for months, and there were several concerns for the Allies. The British in particular were worried about the safety of the prisoners of war, believing that without a Japanese surrender all prisoners might be killed. The Americans, meanwhile, were concerned about the masses of troops who might be lost in combat, not to mention the economic problems that would be encountered, should the war turn into a prolonged affair, Scientists, for the most part, had their own agenda based on curiosity. Nobody knew for certain quite how much devastation could be caused by the atomic bomb. The Japanese refusal to surrender offered an ideal opportunity to test this new weapon of mass destruction.

For all these reasons the first atomic bomb was dropped on Hiroshima on 6 August 1945 at 8.15a.m. It weighed 9,000 lb, and was transported by a B-29 Superfortress piloted by Colonel Tibbets. An eyewitness account described the flash as blinding:

I can't make you understand how bright that flash was. It was a blue flash and it had a ringing sound. It went through you just like the shock you get from an electric battery. It was terribly hot as well, just like solid heat coming at you. We watched the light turn into a yellow glow. It was like sunlight coming from half a dozen suns instead of one. There were yellow rainbows following each other, rippling up above where the bomb had dropped. In the centre there was this column of smoke going up.

While members of the Japanese government were still considering their reaction to Hiroshima, a second bomb was dropped on Nagasaki three days later. The combined death toll of both bombs was 240,000, while thousands more suffered the effects of radiation sickness. The Japanese Emperor Hirohito stepped in to negotiate peace with the Allies. Mountbatten accepted the unconditional surrender of the Japanese in South-east Asia and Singapore on 29 August 1945, while MacArthur accepted the Japanese surrender in Tokyo Bay on 2 September. Hirohito was not tried for war crimes, but he was forced to renounce any claim to his previously unchallenged divine status. Prime minister Tojo, however, was tried as a war criminal and was executed by hanging in 1948. The imprisoned nurses heard the news of the Japanese defeat in various ways. Dame Margot remembers that:

Shortly after that, we had a message that everyone would walk to a hall and we would go there, and the Japanese captain stood on the table and had a translator to say, "The war is over. We are all now friends. We will send you in more supplies." We had heard so many false rumours that it was very difficult to believe it, but that's how we first heard. Later on an allied plane flew over the camp and dropped bread. That was the first bread that we had tasted for three and a half years, just a little portion to divide through the camp.

Phyllis Thoms described the way in which she realised that the Japanese had been defeated:

We had a roll call every day and we weren't allowed out of our buildings until we had given our roll call. So we waited and waited and nothing happened. Then in the middle of the morning apparently the interpreter came in and told the British administrator that we were no longer at war. We were now friends! And we were all issued with a roll of lavatory paper, which we called the "victory roll" because we had been very short of that as you can imagine.

Brenda MacDuff recalled the period of release in her wartime diary:

Two days after we heard on August 25th that peace had been declared came very bad news for the Dutch women who had husbands in the POW camp at Pankanbaru, some 50 miles from us. Out of our 4,500 men 700 had died: there had been a very bad outbreak of typhoid, and now at the end of this internment many found that they were widows. A day or two later several "Red Berets" arrived in our camp. They had been flown in from Colombo and parachuted near several of the camps. What a marvellous sight they were. Tall, young and so healthy looking and most efficient too. Soon lots of food came flying into the camp. They told us that the British men in the Dutch civilian camp were in a very poor state — worse than us. They got them down by train to Padang Hospital and we British (probably 50 of us) were soon to follow.

Not all the camps were easy to locate. Some were deep in the jungle and were so well camouflaged that it was virtually impossible to find them without prior knowledge of their existence. As Gertrude Ramsden, member of the Queen Alexandra's Royal Naval Nursing Service and personal nurse to Lord Louis Mountbatten, recalled:

Even before the surrender ceremony, already seeing the appalling conditions in the prisons, the RAF flew leaflets, medical supplies and food to known camps. Immediately "Sister Ann" the Dakota flew Lady Louis and her rescue team thousands of miles. This historical tour of prisoner of war camps was life saving. Lady Louis at first accompanied by the Director of Medical Services and a secretary were dependent on the Japanese for the location of camps. They met thousands of starving men, bringing them food, medical supplies and hope for their release. She had authority and fortunately the Japanese did as they were told. Her untiring efforts speeded up the rescue operations. So successful were the arrangements that along a front stretching from Burma, Siam, Malaya, Sumatra and Java covering 3,000 miles, within six weeks 90,000 prisoners of war and internees were rescued.

Over 230 camps were found. Medical officers and sisters from military hospitals in India and Ceylon formed part of the rescue services known as RAPWI (Recovery of Allied Prisoners of War and Internees). Their administrative centre was Singapore. In mid-September the other Royal Navy sister and I were flown in a Sunderland to Singapore having offered to help. On arrival Lady Louis suggested we report to the military hospital which was crowded with ex POWs. There I helped to nurse over 130 Indian troops, all in one ward and suffering from advanced tuberculosis; Lucy was caring for civilian patients, who were mentally and physically ill as a result of their internment.

The reaction to the Japanese surrender had been the immediate declaration of the "Republic of

Indonesia" by the Javanese. They hung banners, paraded, and threatened a nationalist movement if the Dutch colonists returned to claim their country. Fighting in the streets made it dangerous for the women and children crowded in camps to return to their homes.

On the 28th of September we flew with six Red Cross welfare workers into Batavia. There we saw the handful of British officers, helped by ex POWs administering a city using Japanese troops. They were distributing food and doing guard duties as willing subordinates. We were then taken to Tjideng camp to meet those caring for the sick in an improvised hospital. The horror of seeing over 9,000 Dutch women and children crowded together, with over a hundred in each bungalow had to be seen to be believed. Suffering from general malnutrition, wasted, scantily clad, anxious for news and still hungry, they found us a novelty.

In addition to the malnutrition and appalling conditions, there was also evidence to suggest that the British fears for the safety of Allied prisoners of war were well founded.

A young South African who came over after the war said he was sure there was another camp. He kept insisting and they did eventually find us, but not until the 10th of September. But they were going to get rid of us. They found papers in the camp. We often wondered if they were going to line us up and shoot us or what they were going to do.

I subsequently learnt that, if they hadn't got the atom bomb, we had eight days to live — that we were all going to be annihilated in groups. They found all the lists. So I must say that the atom bomb saved a tremendous lot of allied prisoners' lives.

The Japanese prison guards were fearful of Allied retribution for the way in which they had treated their women prisoners. In a desperate attempt to make the women look better, they issued all of them with bright red lipsticks. But no amount of make-up could disguise the fact that all of the women were worn down by malnutrition and exhaustion. In fact, the red lipstick simply highlighted their terrible condition. One nurse did decide to don a pair of silk stockings she had managed to save for the final Allied victory and her own much welcomed release: "A young woman from a newspaper came up and saw us — she was very excited to see us. This girl from the *Daily Mail* or *Daily Mirror* looked at this woman's legs and said, 'Good gracious, you are wearing silk stockings.' So this girl said, 'I kept them for the day of days!'"

In the aftermath of victory, however, it was difficult for some of the released nurses to recover any sense of normality. Years of deprivation, humiliation and lack of privacy had taken their toll.

The first few days I wanted to feel like a normal human being, like they were. I found it extremely difficult in one way because I was so nervous, having been hemmed in for so many years behind barbed wire, always surrounded by so many hundreds of people, and longing for a bit of privacy but, when it came to it, I found it was very difficult. I was all right in my brother's house and his wife was very sweet and kind, but I was afraid to go out by myself. I was afraid to answer the telephone. When I went to the shops for the first time I couldn't ask for what I wanted and I had to come out again. I went to the Post Office and couldn't think what I wanted. I found it most difficult.

It is not surprising, and quite understandable, that some nurses harboured a deep resentment of the way in which they had been treated. Gertrude Ramsden commented that, "Yes, I am afraid I am not a Christian — and I still don't like them. I won't buy a Japanese car and I won't buy a Japanese sewing machine. Some of them were very nice. The interpreter was a Christian Japanese and some of them were charming. So I think there are good and bad in every nation. I still thought that the Emperor made a very truculent speech at the end of the war and I must say that I don't go out of my way, but I like to keep away from the subject. I think its best."

Some nurses, like Dame Margot Turner, bore no grudge whatsoever, choosing instead to get back to work as soon as possible and put the past firmly behind them. By 1946 Dame Margot was back working on the wards in England and was awarded the MBE, before being posted to Benghazi in 1947 and to Cyprus in 1948. In 1950 she was promoted to major and in 1956 she was awarded the RRC medal. Eventually, Dame Margot became the Matron-in-Chief of the QAs and Director of the Army Nursing Services in 1964, and received the DBE in 1965. Other nurses may not have acquired the same high professional profile as Dame Margot, but they were able to continue with their careers long after their ordeal at the hands of the Japanese.

There is no doubt that the imprisoned nurses had displayed tremendous courage, and their release from suffering was heartily welcomed in the nursing press. In December 1945 the *British Journal of Nursing* expressed the following sentiments, which clearly reflect the opinions of the times, as well as demonstrating unequivocally the strength of feeling against the Japanese as the perpetrators of many appalling wartime atrocities:

All women who have had the privilege to wear the uniform of a trained nurse hail with sincere rejoicings that noble band whose release from the hands of a murderous crew of inhuman wretches comes after three and a half years of imprisonment, yet who face life with unbroken and unquenchable spirit. The revolting brutalities perpetrated on helpless white enemies, men and women alike, show so similar a pattern of sadistic bestiality that the system must have been originated by those who held power in Japan. We hear of the thirty Australian nurses who were machine-gunned to their death while still in the water, wading ashore after their ship had been torpedoed.

The revelations coming in from day to day of callous torture, of electric current playing on wet, nude bodies, of strenuous, continuous work on starvation diet among malaria infested country, will make everyone who refuses to face the issue, acknowledge that the Japanese race is sub-human; beyond the pale of civilisation.

To the lasting honour of those few nurses who have survived among the 65 who were evacuated from Singapore, February 1942, just before it fell, they retained their courage and integrity, their desire to help those worse off than themselves, their sense of decency and humour during unspeakable mental and physical privations. The epic story may be related as a whole, meantime one must be satisfied to receive it piecemeal. Never has the uniform of a member of the nursing service earned such well deserved credit as it has in innumerable instances in the tragic tumult of 1939 to 1945.

CHAPTER
EIGHT

Picking Up the Pieces

With the cessation of hostilities the focus of both civilian and military organisations shifted towards the reconstruction of normal services and the rehabilitation of the victims of war. Nurses were as instrumental in this process as they had been in the support of the war effort itself. The process of rebuilding, however, was not easy, and the victims of war were more scarred than anyone could have believed possible.

The horrors of the Japanese prisoner of war camps could only be surpassed by the inhumanity of the German concentration camps. As the military nurses approached these camps in April 1945 alongside the fighting forces, nothing could prepare them for the dreadful sights that lay ahead:

Here over an acre of ground, lay dead and dying people. You could not see which was which except, perhaps, by a convulsive movement or the last quiver of a sigh from a living skeleton too weak to move. The living lay with their heads against the corpses. Around them moved the awful, ghostly procession of emaciated, aimless people with nothing to do and no hope of life, unable to move out of your way and unable to look at the sights around them. This day at Belsen was the most horrible of my life.

As Anita Kelly recalled:

We emptied the hospital one evening and, when I came back the next morning the ward was quite full of men from Belsen. There they were with their shaved heads and it was my first experience of the number tattooed on their arm. Very few of them had anywhere to go. They had all lost relatives or whole families in some cases. It was just kindness and patience, tender loving care as it came to be called. But I don't think we had much effect on them. We treated them at the moment for whatever we could. We really couldn't at that time think how these people could possibly pick up the threads of life.

Belsen was only one of many concentration camps established by the Germans for the systematic extermination of Jews. Apart from subjecting Jews to the gas chambers — which were often disguised as communal bathhouses — the German SS doctors carried out many medical and surgical "experiments" on the Jewish prisoners. Other Jewish prisoners were required to undertake hard labour. They worked inhuman hours for little or no food and most died within about nine months of captivity. As the German war effort began to disintegrate, many prisoners were evacuated from the eastern border and marched west: most of these died on the road, too exhausted to reach the other camps. The Germans made vain attempts to cover up the true nature and purpose of the camps, but to no avail. It was impossible to conceal the mass extermination of the Jewish population. Correct figures on the numbers of Jews who were exterminated in camps are not available. An estimated 18 million were incarcerated, and the Germans intended to kill at least 11 million of these. A million, if not more, died as a result of hard labour and deliberate neglect. Historians generally estimate that the number of deaths totalled between 6 and 8 million, although this may fall far short of the truth.

Most of the camps became infamous because of the cruel nature of their leaders, and there is plenty of evidence to suggest that German women officers were every bit as cruel as their male counterparts. As the Allies approached the camps, however, the camp commandants were forced to flee or risk being executed for war crimes. The German commandant of Belsen actually negotiated a British takeover of the camp before the official German surrender, primarily because he feared the risk of a typhus epidemic in rural Germany.

The German commandant of Belsen felt with the oncoming British forces the first thing that would happen would be this great rush of people. He had 60,000 men, women and children prisoners and, of them, about 15,000 were suffering from typhus. If they had escaped into the countryside the disease would have spread. He was concerned about

Germany but he knew just as well that the allies did not want that sort of thing either. So he contacted the Allied Headquarters and arranged that the British would move in ahead of time and a temporary truce would be declared to allow the British to take over the administration, even though the surrounding countryside was still in German hands.

When we got there we were waiting. There was this German hospital and the mess. We thought we would have to work there and we went inside, but the Germans had moved so quickly. There were patients still on the operating table, bodies in the mortuary and there was a marine officers' mess. There were lunch things on the table and food on the plates. They had just walked out!

Despite their attempts to flee, most German camp commandants were later captured and tried for war crimes. The commandant of Belsen from 1944 onwards was Joseph Kramer. More commonly known as the "Beast of Belsen", he was tried and executed in November 1945. Although others were pursued, tried and executed in a similar fashion, some Nazi commandants and doctors did escape. The notorious Dr Joseph Mengele, who had conducted hundreds of medical experiments on Jews and had been nicknamed the "Angel of Death" as a consequence, escaped to South America. He became one of the most pursued of all war criminals and was eventually assumed to have drowned in Brazil in 1979.

German nurses had also been involved in the execution of Jews. Following orders from Hitler and Nazi administrations in the "Fatherland", they gave Jewish and disabled patients poison on a regular basis. It was not uncommon, therefore, for a German sister to come on duty and decide from an existing list of ward patients who precisely was going to be killed that day. Judgements were made on levels of disability and racial purity, and "undesirables" were quickly and medically eliminated.

The British had long suspected the participation of German nurses in the Jewish extermination programme, though hard evidence was difficult to obtain. As the camps were liberated, however, these same German nurses were forced to help with the care of camp victims. "Actually as the victims were moved from camp to camp they went through a cleansing station. They made the German nurses do this. And they were most scrupulously cleansed, completely shaved and disinfested. Then they were nursed in German barracks there. Anyone with typhus wasn't allowed to leave until they were cured, or most of them died. By the time they were circulating in the countryside they no longer had the typhus."

As the true horrors of the camps were revealed and the news filtered back to Britain, the *British Journal of Nursing* took a hard line on the perpetrators of such inhumanity. In a direct appeal to the professional readership, the paper called for retribution rather than for forgiveness:

We call upon Registered Nurses to stand firm for justice, in so far as the guilty in this war must be punished; we must not let any argument from weak-minded persons divert us from this determination. When the responsible press informs us that Britons were among the tortured in a German camp where 700,000 died it is our bounden duty to punish such inhumanity.

The Evening Standard, a most fearless and patriotic paper reports: The Germans killed a number of British and Americans in extermination camps near Lvov, a special Soviet commission disclosed, said Moscow radio. The commission declared that several Englishmen were killed by "slow torture" at Rava Russkaya camp. "Nearly 700,000 men, women and children were killed by the Germans, including citizens of Czecho-Slovakia, Yugoslavia, Holland, Great Britain and the United States, brought to Lvov from concentration camps in Germany", the commission announced. In addition, 200,000 more were killed in Janow extermination camp.

The statement said that the direct participation of Himmler in these massacres has been definitely established. He personally inspected the executioners. It would be a world disaster if Britain fails to punish these murderers. They should be hanged.

As the postwar rhetoric and "cries for blood" subsided, there were also distinct political efforts to isolate the concept of Nazism from the German people overall. Hitler and Nazi ideology were portrayed as the enemy, and not the bulk of the German population. Besides which, the Allies had other difficulties with which to contend. The control of epidemics had been a major problem for the Allies in all the theatres of war, and this dilemma was only intensified by the subsequent reconstruction period. Polio, diphtheria, typhus and tuberculosis were all significant threats. In an attempt to combat the spread of disease, an alliance was formed between the Red Cross and the Red Crescent Societies of the Soviet Union, and nurses visited over 10,000 villages giving lectures on health, hygiene and nutrition. Some of the equipment necessary for the health education programme was provided by the American Red Cross. Moreover, there was a consensus between all health organisations that epidemics needed to be curtailed at the earliest opportunity. The *British Journal of Nursing* announced that: "The campaign against epidemics reported by E.J. Pampana, MD, Director of Health and Relief Bureau, proves that: "It is wiser as well to erect a parapet along the top of a dangerous cliff than to provide an ambulance at the base." . . . It should never be forgotten that the education of the public is a very important factor, upon which the success of any health campaign — and still more that of an anti-epidemic campaign — depends to a large extent."

Although epidemics were a major and widespread concern, malnutrition too was a big problem and food advice centres were established in an attempt to supplement poor food supplies. In December 1945 a Red Cross Commission formed a team of health-care professionals and set out to alleviate the situation in Berlin. They distributed "artic packs", which comprised concentrated foods originally destined for British troops undergoing manoeuvres in sub-artic conditions. Since they were no longer needed by the troops, the British decided to add the contents of the packs to the rations of Berlin children up to the age of fourteen. But the process of establishing food advice centres was difficult and was hampered by staff shortages. The German knowledge of nutrition seemed extremely poor and the distribution of new knowledge even poorer, as the following extract from a report written by Rose Simmonds, registered nurse and dietician, and Elsie Stephenson, registered nurse and health visitor, explained:

Berlin is, at present, far behind London in respect of food advice centres, though in the American sector there is an Institute of Nutritional Research, the only one of its kind in Germany, where wild herbs are cultivated and tested for their nutritional values, and afterwards cooked from recipes drawn up by scientific workers. These recipes are then sent to the magistrate, but as there are only a few food advice centres, they only reach comparatively few housewives. The British, French and Russian sectors have only one advice centre each, and until the end of May there was no such centre in the American sector. The team visited the food advice centre in the Russian zone, where they attended an excellent demonstration showing how to eke out flour ration, and how to recognise and prepare for the table, wild herbs of good nutritional value. A dish of chickweed, combined with lime leaves tasted rather like spinach. Barley, roasted for various lengths of time in different degrees of heat yielded various different flavours. Flour made from horse chestnuts made excellent cakes, and an infusion of pine needles contained a fair amount of vitamin C.

The present shortage of premises and suitable teachers is holding up the work of the Institutes, as formerly, many of the domestic science teachers were members of the Nazi party, and since their dismissal, others cannot be found to take their places.

The people of Berlin were, on the whole, less depressed than the team had expected. Some showed a definite defeatist attitude, others professed themselves as profoundly shocked by the enforced lowered standard of living; but some were sincerely trying to work out schemes for the rehabilitation of their social and welfare services. It must be remembered that the Germans, geared up for many years to victory over the whole world, have suffered an overwhelming psychological shock, and how this will affect the coming generation is at present unpredictable. The fact remains that help is needed at this time towards the rehabilitation of youth groups, to be conducted on non-political lines, and if possible an early exchange of young German students with those of other countries.

In addition to the endeavours of the Red Cross, the World Health Organisation (WHO) and similar bodies made every effort to resettle all refugees and victims of war. Among the nurses working with the United Nations Relief and Rehabilitation Administration (UNRRA) to achieve this goal was Monica Baly, whose experience of war had given her a new outlook on the nursing and medical profession. "I resolved that once I was demobbed I would retrain as a health visitor. I wasn't going back to hospital. I realized that so much ill health was preventable. But the war made me. It taught me what I could do. It gave me courage in fact to do the things I could do. You just had to get on and do things, and it's by getting on and doing things that you find out what you can do." In the postwar years Monica became a Royal College of Nursing representative for the south-west of England, and spent much of her time striving to improve hospital and community conditions for nurses and patients alike. In later years she became a tutor on the nursing degree course and wrote the basic set book for the course. Not content with this, in her retirement Monica gained her PhD, wrote books and gave lectures about nursing history; she was still writing up to her death in 1998.

For all the military nurses who were demobbed at the end of the war the process of returning to civilian life required a considerable period of adjustment. The mundane "run of the mill" hospital routines seemed dull after their adventures abroad. Nurse Kitchener expressed the sentiments of many demobbed nurses in the following letter, written from Queen Mary's Hospital, Carshalton:

214

I have been very busy settling into civilian life after six years in the army, I returned to my old post as ward sister and find the children a great change after the men. I miss the moves of the army as I travelled quite a long way, Norway, M.E.F., Palestine and Egypt, France and Belgium. I was extremely pleased to see so much of Palestine especially Jerusalem and was lucky enough to meet my brother who was over with the Australian army. I had not seen him for 15 years so we had a grand meeting.

I went over to France five weeks after D-day, and wallowed in mud and rain (we were in a tented hospital) for weeks before we moved into Belgium, a most interesting two-day journey in lorries. My posting to Germany came at the same time as my release. I was awfully sorry not to go.

Not all military nurses were able to return to their old posts, however, and the RCN issued a pamphlet offering guidance to the demobbed nurses. The pamphlet was tinged with words of caution, since members of the college recognised that the return to civilian nursing would involve disappointment for the many who had risen high in the ranks of military life.

When you come out of the forces you will have eight weeks in which to look round and take stock of your position. After the first wonderful weeks of reunion and rest, you will want to think about your plans for the future. You have seen much, and you will want to bring to civilian life a broadened

215

outlook. It may be that during your period of service you concentrated on one special branch of nursing work, while possibly losing touch with developments in other fields. Perhaps you have held posts of great responsibility.

While you have been away, those at home have had to carry on as best they could with sadly depleted ranks; so of one thing you can be certain: the civilian nursing service desperately needs your help. Many older nurses, whether in administrative positions or among the rank and file, have held on month by month, waiting for your return to enable them to enjoy their long deferred retirement. The vacancies are many, and, if you have qualities of leadership, the big posts at home will be yours in the end; but do not be disappointed if, because you have held a position of authority in the field, you do not step straight into a similar position at home. Not everyone who has risen to a matronship in His Majesty's Forces can hope for an immediate matron's post in civilian life.

The statement holds a wonderful irony in that it was not the military nurses who were out of touch with new nursing techniques and developments but their civilian counterparts. New innovations in drug therapy, such as penicillin, had not yet even reached civilian hospitals. Techniques with regard to blood transfusions, physiotherapy, burns, chest injuries, and a host of other treatments had moved rapidly forward in the military nursing sector, leaving the civilian field far behind.

Consequently, the newly demobbed nurses were streets ahead of their civilian colleagues when it came to the latest medical and nursing developments.

This situation led to some amusing incidents on the civilian hospital wards. There were cases where demobbed nurses were getting patients out of bed soon after their operations, only to find the very same patients hurried back into bed by long-established civilian nurses. The latter were convinced that patients would die if they were moved out of their beds so soon after surgery. Of course, the ex-military nurses knew that this would not be the case, and that early ambulation actually prevented post-operative complications rather than causing them, but it was not easy to assure their colleagues of this fact. The war on the wards continued, therefore, with demobbed nurses fighting a losing battle, unable to implement many of the new techniques that had been discovered as a result of medical and nursing experience during the war.

Nor had the military nurse struggle for officer status been clearly or accurately interpreted by civilian registered nurses. They believed that identification with the "officer class" merely confirmed their membership of an elite social class and endorsed their authority over less qualified nurses. Others within the profession adopted a broader interpretation of this status and argued that "officer" nurses should ideally possess similar character traits to those normally required for military leadership. The RCN established a Reconstruction Committee chaired by Lord Horder, which produced reports in 1942, 1943 and 1949. Horder stressed that "officer class" nurses were essential in order to stimulate professional development. According to Horder, the main function of officer class nurses (who he recognised as being the registered nurses) was to provide professional leadership. But it was precisely this aspect of the "officer" status that the majority of civilian nurses failed to grasp, and it was this failure that highlighted the civilian distortion of the modern military nursing model.

Subsequently, this distortion impeded professional progress as civilian nurses were left with the "dead hand" of an outdated Nightingale military nursing model. Despite their failure to take hold of the realities of the military officer role, civilian nurses continued to be obsessed with the symbolic trappings of military protocol. Uniforms, parades, badges, stripes, ceremonial procedures and overt racism were all military features that had been incorporated into the civilian nursing profession. At times, nurses even formed a guard of honour for visiting dignitaries. Such was the degree of institutional racism, for example, that in 1948 the Minister of Health "dissociated himself from the action of a London matron who imposed a colour bar at a dance in respect of one of her own nursing staff, a colonial citizen working in the best interest of the London community". Unfortunately, this action by a matron was not an isolated incident and, while the shortage of nurses necessitated the use of immigrant labour, matrons did not always respect immigrant nurses as equal members of the workforce. The hierarchy of races was visible in the recruitment practices of most hospitals, with black and Irish nurses appearing at the bottom of the hierarchical order.

In addition to the problems associated with racism, authoritarian paramilitary rule continued to dominate civilian nursing practice, and an accompanying anti-educational bias endorsed the aristocratic neo-feudalist military belief that a person's character was more important than their intellect and that, therefore, nurses were born not made. The nursing establishment refused to contemplate any reform of nurse training, and rejected the logical recommendation to separate the education of nurses from nursing service that appeared in the government-initiated Wood Report of 1947. The GNC insisted that nurse training should remain as a practical-based apprentice-style system. As a result, yet another irony emerged, whereby the GNC, having rejected educational reform, consistently lobbied the government to reinstate the minimum educational qualification for nurse training.

There were, of course, senior nurses in Whitehall who had agitated for reform, but these nurses were far outnumbered by conservative and domineering matrons. Despite intense opposition from the latter group, it was now abundantly clear that even the patients were beginning to recognise the need for action in the field of civilian nursing. One severely dissatisfied patient wrote a lengthy letter to a Miss Goodchild, who was doing her best to elevate civilian nurse status. The letter was published in the nursing press and highlighted some of the problems affecting patient care and nursing standards:

Dear Miss Goodchild,

Having read about your campaign to protect the interests of the Nursing Profession, and thereby those who are likely to be in need of nursing care, I wanted to wish you every possible success in your endeavours to ensure that a professional status in nursing will receive its just reward and a full share of dignity.

It is very gratifying to read that a matron has at last taken up the cudgels to fight the evils which are besetting the profession. I do not think that people realise how serious they are. Only when people of your rank in the profession take up these matters will anything be done. I only hope that more responsible people will assist you to voice the state of affairs. Perhaps my own experience will encourage you even further in your convictions. They are so right.

I was unfortunate enough to be stricken with tuberculosis whilst in the Navy, and very fortunately for me I was treated in the Brompton Hospital where I found the hospital was all that it should be in dealing with disease. I did not know what it was to lack confidence either in the medical men or the nursing staff.

Unfortunately the disease attacked my spine and I was sent to a small orthopaedic hospital in my own home county. I was utterly shocked at the state of affairs which prevailed here, and from what I have since heard there are similar places up and down the country. The "Cinderella" hospitals just cannot obtain the required standards in their staff. These are the existing example of the menace of the system which does not include the recognised entry of nurses into hospital and subsequent training.

My disease did not distress me half so much as the hell of being at the mercy of such very undesirable people. For the most part the staff consisted of orderlies, untrained nurses, part time assistant nurses; male nurses occasionally came on duty to help with the women's block.

The orderlies could scarcely have been worse. Many were shiftless, idle and dirty. Working with them discouraged young cadet nurses and student nurses, many of whom left the profession and were lost to it for good.

There were eternal arguments mainly arising out of what one could well name "differentials". A patient would ask for a bedpan and a nurse would probably walk all along the block to tell an orderly, in turn, the orderly would say it was not in her list of duties to give bedpans. The nurse would argue that the orderly was paid to do that task. I use this as a simple illustration of the indiscipline which can arise.

We had one orderly, a male, who had been a mental patient, and was entirely misplaced on the ward. I do not need to describe the annoyances we suffered from him.

Another female orderly was so filthy she would go ahead to the preparation of food in the midst of giving urinals or bedpans. Her hands had to be seen to be believed. I cannot describe the misery of such a place, and there are many who share my views. At all costs this element should be kept out of the hospitals or in their proper perspective — doing merely domestic work. I for one would rejoice if nurses were given the pay the orderlies get and the latter reduced to a bare minimum. When one meets a good orderly they usually are good, but alas the shiftless ones outnumber these.

By and large, my experience was that many of them were not even clean in their persons and the language they resorted to to the younger nursing staff was not calculated to encourage good relations.

My two years on my back were a nightmare to me because I had to suffer such things. In the middle of it all I had to have my gall bladder removed and was sent to the nearby infirmary. There was a pleasure in the midst of pain — the clean wards, the efficient kind sister, and staff nurse, were wonderful after my past experience and I hated to go back to the orthopaedic hospital.

Because some of these people had no knowledge of proper serving of food to patients meal times were often revolting. Dirty cutlery, crockery, and the food thrown on, any old how. (I may tell you that we hadn't even a ward sister at this hospital for three months, a young student nurse was trying to administer the ward.)

I have since told professional friends and they can hardly believe what I tell them, except those who came and saw for themselves. I know many fine women who uphold the best traditions of nursing who have been horrified at what I tell them.

There are many "therapy" careers which now attract those girls who would normally have gone in for nursing. With County Council grants, and local educational grants these careers are becoming available to all of intelligence. Nursing should not be dragged down by the inception of this new scheme which you are fighting; or it will not attract even the numbers it does now.

If only the wives of people in authority or the relatives of such people could have a glimpse of the second era of "Dickens" characters which have already got into some of the hospitals something would be done. Ignorance I feel is the cause and the fact that many sisters and matrons will not rise up in protest but "make do" with this very poor material. A patient who complains is very often unpopular. I complained loudly and many things were altered but the situation was so bad that nothing short of dismissing the entire staff and recruiting a new one would have righted matters.

Nobody takes much notice of the "difficult tubercular" patients as you probably know, as we are notoriously temperamental, so the weapons left to fight with were few. I may say my nervous state was infinitely worse than any physical ills at the end of two years.

I may say that I know hospitals very well having worked as a VAD in the Royal Navy during the war, and training as an occupational therapist afterwards. These posts enabled me to see the best in the service to patients. Our discipline was strict and work hard in the Navy — I was appalled at the laziness of the people I met when I was ill with my spinal ailment. Their lack of medical ethics was terrible. One heard of night staff orderlies talking loudly on buses of patients' private affairs and as they had access to the records of patients a great deal of discussion went on which was highly irregular.

I'm afraid I have been very long-winded. I wanted you to know what a grand thing you will be doing if you succeed in your endeavours. My experience is one of many and it was most bitter. I wish you the best of luck in your crusade. I was delighted to learn that you are trying to effect these very necessary reforms.

[signed] S.W.

Miss Goodchild was actually a matron at the Christie Hospital, and Holt Radium Institute, Manchester, when this letter was written, and her crusade was mainly a protest at a government decision to recognise the grade of nursing auxiliary as a person who is "engaged wholly or mainly on nursing duties". Again, this was a move by a senior member of the profession to reassert the status of the registered nurse above that of the assistant and auxiliary nurse. In view of the existing labour shortages, it was a protest that was entirely inappropriate. Instead of complaining about the poor quality of nursing orderlies and auxiliaries and their relative status to registered nurses, action that was more relevant and constructive was needed.

At this time, there were no official training courses for orderlies or auxiliaries in any hospitals. If they were lucky they might have received a couple of days' instruction in bedmaking and cleaning lockers. Since these people formed the bulk of the nursing workforce, along with student nurses, a sensible course of action would have been to ensure that these lower grades received adequate training to administer basic care to patients. If these grades were not taught basic hygiene standards and food preparation, how were they supposed to learn? The fact was that the nursing profession did not want these lower grades to be trained in case this process undermined their own registered nurse status. Consequently, some patients suffered substandard nursing care simply because the nursing profession was more concerned with protecting professional interests than with providing adequate nursing care.

Thus the very same problems that had deterred nurse recruitment during the war years continued unabated. As the nursing profession entered the NHS, over 30,000 beds were closed because of nursing shortages. As Lord Shepherd stated in the House of Lords:

More hospital beds are now occupied than before the war and many thousands are awaiting admission. There has been an increase of over 170,000 births per annum since 1940, which means that many more midwives are needed. The demand

225

for nurses for other fields — e.g. industrial nursing and school nursing — has greatly increased. The armed forces even in peacetime have to make greater calls upon trained personnel in this field than they used to make, and there are overseas civilian needs which have to be met, in Europe, in the Colonies and elsewhere.

This statement was not entirely correct in that the nursing complement of the armed forces was actually being reduced to prewar numbers, rather than being increased. In addition, the armed forces organised the early release of nursing personnel in an attempt to ease the civilian situation, and there were concerted efforts to try to persuade men to enter general nursing, although these efforts were not introduced without some reservations. As Lord Crook announced in the House of Lords during a debate on the nursing crisis:

I stand here in the very difficult role of advocating the employment of male nurses while being quite certain that I like having had my brow smoothed by a ministering angel of the female sex. So we share that view of nursing. I regret that the economic situation and the manpower situation of the country forces me to suggest such outrageous things as taking away ministering angels and substituting male nurses.

This view was echoed by other members of the House of Lords:

Men nurses for mental cases and for other specialised forms of attention of course are quite right; but I do not know about general nursing. Perhaps it is only the sentimental attitude of a man who, fortunately, in his own case is hardly ever ill, but I am inclined to think that I would get better more quickly if I too had a ministering angel of the female sex. I question whether even the best trained man would do quite as well for me.

The *British Journal of Nursing* presented another view:

For many years now women have struggled to gain equality with men in the world of employment. In all the long bitter struggle there has been one sphere where the right of employment was never questioned — the nursing profession. Inevitably, it seems, with the reshuffling of the sexes in the employment world, men have come knocking at the doors of the nursing profession. We can look on with sympathy, albeit with some amusement, to see the reversal of the struggles we have so long participated in.

Men will have to realise that to compete with women in their own sphere other than at a time of shortage of candidates, will not be easy for them. Men will have to realise more than they seem to do now, that there is more to ward management than the treatment of the patients, before they will be a serious threat to women's supremacy as ward sisters. If men could bring into their wards the order and cleanliness of a crack ship as well as their noted thoroughness, any matron would have a charge nurse to delight her.

The government had stressed that an extra 50,000 nurses were needed in order to staff the forthcoming NHS, and Lord Crook in the nursing crisis debate had "referred to the tyrants of matrons under whom the poor students had to work, and to the wrongness of the cloistered life of the sister, and of the matrons who were brought up the hard way, and made it their duty to see that new students were brought up likewise". Lord Crook also gave numerous examples of the shoddy way in which new nurses were treated by senior members of their profession.

The government, too, emphasised the need for civilian matrons to loosen their hold over the lives of student nurses. In a Ministry of Labour pamphlet the government asserted that, "The staffing of a hospital can be seriously prejudiced by bad staff relations, e.g. inadequate training methods, the 'institutional' attitude of senior staff, repressive discipline, out-moded social distinctions between grades of staff especially between trained and student nurses and between part-time and full-time staff, and restrictions on the personal freedom of nurses when off duty."

Even the militarising Matron-in-Chief spoke out against the excessive nurse discipline: "If the public has any complaint against the nursing profession, it is of its over-rigidity of discipline, and exaggerated differential status. We, who know hospital life from the inside, can justify many practices which seem stilted, petty, and old-fashioned to outsiders. But I think we shall agree that some of these criticisms are not without justification." The nursing profession, however, failed to take heed.

Despite the severe nursing shortages caused by this petty and oppressive discipline, traditional prejudices against male nurses were difficult to overcome. Although official statistics suggested that one in five nurses were male in 1949, as compared with one in ten before the war, these statistics did not separate the mental nursing sector from the general, or the trained from the untrained staff. According to the GNC figures for 1945, the number of general nurses registered by examination consisted of 7,157 females and only 29 men. Even taking into account the intensive courses introduced by the government to encourage demobilised men into the general nursing field, it was some time before they were able to make any impact on the female-dominated general nursing sector, although there were a significant number of surgeons who, immediately the war was over, demanded that the theatres should once again be run by men rather than by women. But when the matron of the Royal London Hospital did appoint two men to do just this task after the war, they abandoned their posts after only six months, claiming that they had found the work far too strenuous. It was with some glee that the matron informed the surgeons of this fact, and the women were reinstated.

It was also clear that the recently demobbed nurses who had worked alongside male RAMC orderlies during the war were perfectly amenable to accepting male nurses within the field of general nursing practice. The opposition to men came not from those working at ward level but from those women who were in the higher echelons of nursing society. Consequently, the RCN did not admit men into its ranks until 1960, and major London teaching hospitals did not accept them for general nurse training until 1966.

But, if the members of the civilian nursing service were beleaguered by traditional prejudices against immigrants and men, low status, an outdated military style training system and professional stagnation, at least the military nursing service fared better. At the end of the war, the salaries of military nurses were initially aligned with the civilian Rushcliffe pay scales, but these were deemed inappropriate for military officers and were rejected. Instead, military nurses successfully lobbied the Ministry of Defence to affirm their position within the Army vis-à-vis the Women's Royal Army Corps (WRAC), formerly the ATS, and to adjust their pay scales accordingly. A memorandum from the Secretary of State for War explained that:

The QARANC will have powers of command over all women at all times and all men placed under their command. They will be subject to the Army Act as will the WRAC. They do not understand why they should be the only class of officer, male or female, whose emoluments and conditions of service are directly based on those of civilians. They cannot be expected to be satisfied with different and inferior conditions of service, such as the lack of time promotion, from those of WRAC officers with whom they will serve side by side.

The Minister of Health eventually acknowledged that higher salaries were justified for military nurses because of their position as officers of the armed forces. Their salary scales, therefore, were adjusted to conform with that of other women officers. But military nurses were still not satisfied. They argued that, since all nurses were more qualified than WRAC officers when they entered military service, they should receive adequate recompense for these qualifications. After a period of considerable negotiation, the Ministry of Defence agreed to award the nurses a "professional lead" in salary terms over other military women. Thus the military nursing services had successfully asserted their position, and had claimed a salary lead over both the civilian nursing services and fellow military women. However, all military women, including nurses, were paid less than their male colleagues.

As a result of postwar negotiations the Queen Alexandra's Imperial Military Nursing Service had become the Queen Alexandra's Royal Army Nursing Corps (QARANC). The other military nursing services followed suit and established their own corps. Military nurses had, at last, secured their place within the service framework. Arrangements were made with the GNC that would enable military matrons to recruit and train women for nurse registration within the armed forces, rather than relying on the recruitment of nurses who had already been trained in the civilian hospitals. For this purpose a new QARANC training headquarters was established at Hindhead on 13 September 1950. The QAs were also afforded their own "march-past" tune entitled "Grey and Scarlet", which was designed to emphasise their role as soldier and nurse and to fit in with military tradition. Their ranks conformed to those of the Army generally.

Thus the status of military nurses continued to outstrip civilian nurses, and this was reflected in recruitment statistics. As the *British Journal of Nursing* revealed in 1946:

We learn that while hospitals are finding great difficulty in recruiting nurses, applications greatly in excess of vacancies are being received by the nursing services of the Royal Navy, Army and RAF. All these nurses are granted officer status. Travel and distinctive uniforms are further attractions. Only 109 of the 455 nurses applying can be accepted by the Queen Alexandra's Imperial Military Nursing Service, as the service is being reduced from the peak wartime figure of 12,000 to its normal complement of 624. For 11 vacancies in Queen Alexandra's Royal Naval Nursing Service nearly 60 nurses are competitors.

So the low status of civilian nursing continued to favour recruitment to the military sector, and this existing trend was highlighted by the arrival of the NHS. By virtue of her officer status, the military nurse was able to gain some degree of political leverage within the military framework; the civilian nurse had no such leverage. Even before the arrival of the NHS, nurses were voicing their concern over the possible erosion of the matron's power. Some nurses believed that this erosion was a form of poetic justice for not opposing the 1943 Nurses Act. In 1945 the nursing press reported that:

> Criticism of the present system of nurse control has appeared in several leading papers during the past month. Depreciation of the matron's power is thinly veiled by medical superintendents. What with sister tutors, dieticians, college wardens and other officers, it would appear the matron is a back number. The fact that as a powerful body of 1,000 strong, they did not unite to prevent the degrading of nursing standards, is widely resented by many registered nurses, especially those in private practice.

Those nurses who had expressed fears that the NHS would further downgrade the power of the matron and the nursing voice overall were correct in their assessment. The *British Journal of Nursing* commented on the matter in 1948:

> Overnight the management of our hospitals passed from autonomy to centralism. The central administrators bear a heavy responsibility, and it is to be hoped that they keep a level head and pause

well before sweeping aside established customs, for it is far easier to destroy than build. We are all anxious to see our National Health Service stand eventually second to none in the world, but we are also anxious that we abate not one jot of our present standards. It is so easy, in a change of management, to go through chaos before reaching perfection, through too hasty a change of regime. The nursing profession has a large part to play in the success of a national scheme. It is disquieting, therefore, to find that nursing has very little representation on the regional boards and few local management committees have appointed a nurse member.

Failure to establish the nursing voice and take control of professional direction within the early stages of NHS development had serious repercussions for civilian nurses. For over a decade, their nurse leaders were unable to influence policy decisions and their concerns were swallowed up among other health-care professionals. By rejecting the reform of nurse education they had effectively closed the door on professional advancement. As the International Council of Nurses noted in 1947: "It was felt by many people that the present system of nursing education was not always of the type that produced leaders of the ward unit, the hospital unit in the public health field or of the profession as a whole. In this last especially, there lies a danger that the profession may not always be organised for the greater participation in and contribution to the health service of the people."

It was not until the Salmon administrative reforms were implemented from 1970 onwards that the nursing voice was reinstated, and nurses moved more confidently in the direction of education. Salmon also conferred the title "officer" on senior civilian nurses. But, although in their efforts to gain status throughout the war civilian nurses had continually identified with the military and masculinity, their status could not be sustained by this process. As the leading protagonist of nurse militarisation Dame Katherine Jones had noted in 1944, "Status cannot be created or justified by such military scaffolding alone." It was nearly thirty years before the civilian nursing profession finally acknowledged the validity of this statement.

By contrast, the military nursing corps embraced education and professional development with open arms. As a consequence, "Senior officers from the various nursing corps were among the leaders in creating what has become institutionalised as the Brussels-based Senior Women Officers Committee within NATO. At the time of its formation in the early 1970s nursing officers were the highest-ranking women throughout the North American and Western European forces."

For her part, Dame Katherine Jones was able to retire from military service in the certain knowledge that the long and hard fight she had undertaken had achieved its aim to obtain adequate recognition for her nurses. The commissioned officer status awarded to all military registered nurses had provided a firm basis for their postwar negotiations with the Ministry of Defence, and for military nursing development. Dame Katherine, who had essentially adopted the "if you can't beat them, join them" approach to military service, explained the "method in her madness" to the Association of Hospital Matrons in her retirement, and concluded that:

After 27½ years in the army I am now a civilian and, for the last few weeks, I have been able to look at this question more as a nurse than as a soldier, and perhaps in time I shall think less of rank, badges and uniform and the significance of officer status. I do not know yet, but this I do know: I shall not fail to recognise at once in civilian as in military nursing any of the straws which show which way the wind is blowing on the fortunes of our profession. I shall always be jealous for the dignity of the nursing profession. I shall always be pernickety about the symbols of its rank. I shall always be a tiger on its behalf and a devotee in support of all efforts for its improvement. At the same time I shall cherish the hope that some day a generation of state registered nurses will be able to live in a community where their status is assured, their importance unchallenged, and their conditions of work worthy of their service to humanity. Only then will the British nursing profession be able to give us nursing at its best.

In reality, though, Dame Katherine's "method and madness" approach had only prevailed in the civilian nursing sector because professionalism had failed. Nurses were prevented from taking a professional or educational route to enhance their status, so they adopted a militarisation policy. This endorsement of militarism offered the vain hope that once registered nurses' status was equated with the military "officer class", then the overall status of the professional nurse would be elevated. For a short time this policy worked, and as civilian nurses identified with the concept of military efficiency and masculinity there was at least a shift away from the notion that nurses were merely motherly skivvies. Nevertheless, in the long term, a status based on a hierarchical framework and rigid notions of social and racial injustice could not be sustained. It can also be argued that, by identifying so strongly with the concept of masculine military efficiency, the caring, nurturing aspects of nursing were essentially undermined.

More importantly, the nursing profession's over-identification with the military prevented the much-needed educational reform of the civilian nursing sector. The nursing policies that emanated from the nursing establishment were all driven with status concerns in mind. Most nurses did not envisage a status that was linked to potential educational achievement but one which was rooted in military culture. As nurses became swallowed up within the health-care framework of the NHS, the lack of educational reform held significant implications for their patients. Nurses found that they were often "out of their depth" in relation to new medical innovations. Subsequently, as Monica Baly has noted, "The process of democracy in nursing was delayed because technical knowledge advanced with such rapidity that each generation was stranded on the beach of insecurity."

CHAPTER
NINE

Facing the Future

During the Second World War all unmarried women between the ages of seventeen and forty-five were conscripted and worked in a variety of jobs ranging from anti-aircraft gunners and armament workers to agricultural labourers. But despite their efforts in war, nearly all these women were poorly served in employment terms by postwar society. Many had hoped that job opportunities would expand as a result of their wartime endeavours, but most were still restricted to the same types of work that had been regarded as acceptable for women before the war. While it was true that things had improved in some areas — for instance, the doors of medical schools were now open to women — in most employment fields there was a tendency to drift back to a pre-war patriarchal state. Perhaps the biggest change for women centred on the fact that the "marriage bar" was lifted in the public sector. Before the war, all women were forced to resign their employment positions on marriage, whereas after the war this rule was abolished with the exception of certain positions within the civil service.

Furthermore, although postwar Britain was experiencing severe labour shortages, the government chose to resolve these shortages by embarking on a massive immigration policy rather than by encouraging women into the labour market. Thus countless children's nurseries were closed and government propaganda attempted to persuade women that their rightful place was in the home, although the Ministry of Labour was forced to do an about turn on this policy by 1950 when the true extent of labour shortages was recognised. Nevertheless, the nursing profession had already succumbed to the initial overall trend and was itself relieving shortages by relying on an immigrant labour force rather than introducing flexible work hours and providing creche facilities for existing married nurses.

By the late 1940s, sixteen British colonies had established selection and recruitment procedures to ensure a steady intake of colonial nurse recruits for the NHS. "Enterprising matrons set off to the Caribbean, West Africa and the Philippines to recruit labour. In some cases they were so successful that you could find hospitals where almost all the staff below the rank of sister were of ethnic minority." Immigration was not merely used to alleviate nursing shortages; it was also used by the nursing profession to reinforce existing class distinctions, thereby elevating the position of the registered nurse. Most immigrants were channelled into assistant enrolled nurse training rather than registered nurse training.

Some of these immigrants did not even realise the significance of the different training schemes. As Trevor Clay, the first male president of the RCN, has pointed out, enrolled nurse training represented "one of the health service's biggest confidence tricks. Pupil nurse courses were filled in the 1950s and 1960s by recruits from Mauritius, the Philippines and elsewhere, who were misled into believing they were doing a registered nurse training that would put them on a secure career path. Too late, they discovered that the enrolled nurse qualification was the road to nowhere in the UK and virtually useless back home."

There were no promotional prospects associated with the assistant nurse grade, and registered nurses kept the grade deliberately suppressed just as they had during the war. Consequently, access to power could only be claimed by white middle-class registered nurses. Many hospitals were still so obsessed with status that they flatly refused to run pupil nurse courses. As a senior nurse from Manchester recalled: "They thought they would lose status — the question of status came into it — to a certain extent they just wanted to train State Registered Nurses because it was a higher qualification, and I think they were frightened of the type of girl who would be coming in for State Enrolled training."

But immigrant nurses were not the only ones to be exploited by the civilian nursing profession. The "cadet schemes" that had been established during the war and were supposed to be modelled on the military recruitment practice of "catching them young" continued to thrive until the late 1960s. The quality of such schemes varied enormously between individual hospitals, as did the tasks they were expected to perform. In some hospitals, cadets delivered messages from one department to another and helped with cleaning and sewing, while in others they were acting as anaesthetic nurses keeping an eye on patients until they came round from their operations. The Ministry of Health attempted to introduce guidelines for the employment of cadets but these were difficult to enforce. As Monica Baly recalled, "Most schemes in reality were merely exploiting children."

The Ministry of Health also tried to change the recruitment patterns within the profession by encouraging the notion of part-time employment, while ministers also tried to improve staff relations. But matrons continued to rely on their heroic military past to attract recruits and continued to instil the "character-forming" discipline in their new protégés once they arrived. Campaigns were launched to coincide with Civil Defence weeks and a popular recruitment film, shown nationally to school children in the late 1960s, began with the arrest of Edith Cavell in 1915! Girls were no longer entirely convinced by such films and, as the Headmasters Association acknowledged, were put off by "terrifying stories of untrained nurses being left in charge of wards at night added to long hours and poor pay and the old-fashioned attitudes of some matrons who rule with a rod of iron". Likewise, the National Association of Head Teachers stated bluntly that "neither high ideals nor long-term rewards will attract new recruits into the profession or retain them if they do wish to enter, if actual conditions are poor. The word of mouth gets around and recruitment often stands or falls by word of mouth communication between existing nurses and potential recruits."

Certainly, student nurses still suffered from appalling working conditions. The secretary of the Killearn branch of the Confederation of Health Service Employees summed up the plight of the student nurse in a parody of Kipling's poem "If":

If you can keep your head when all about you
are calling for bottles and pans just from you.
If you can hold your tongue when sister shouts to
    you
and make allowances for her shouting too.

If you can make beds and not be tired from the
    making
and being chased around from morn till night.
If you can keep a smile though your feet are aching
and yet still think your choice of job is right.

If you can dream and still listen to your tutors.
If you can play and not make life a game.
If you can mix with surgeons, doctors, suitors
and treat all these diversions just the same.

If you can bear to hear the one you've tended
torn by pain and gasping just for breath.
Or watch and hold her hand till life is ended
and pray that she will find peace in death.

If you can make one heap of all your wages
and try and budget till next month's due
And fail, and start again on some fresh pages
and make it last the four weeks through.

If you can force your knife through bone and sinew
and make a meal from some old bullock meat
And then get up with nothing in you
Except the bit you've forced yourself to eat.

If you can treat all sorts of wounds and dressings
Yet sympathise and keep the tender touch,
And in all this you find God's many blessings
and all your patients count but none too much.

If you can work each unforgiving minute
and stand each day's long demanding whirl.
Yours is the hospital and everything in it
and what is more you'll be a nurse my girl.

For the British military nurses who, when compared to other women, had largely borne the brunt of wartime horrors the civilian nursing sector was extremely disappointing. Many who had left military service at the end of the war could not bear the thought of re-entering the civilian hospital with all its petty restrictions. They opted instead to work in the public health sector. Of the group who survived the war and are featured in this book, nearly all continued to have distinguished nursing careers. But over 3,000 nurses had died as a result of wartime service (this compares with just over 300 for the ATS), and many more suffered psychological and physical scars as a result of the conflict.

Most believed that their sacrifice had not been adequately acknowledged. While it was true that nurses featured heavily in the New Year's Honours List during the immediate postwar years, and many received medals for their heroic achievements, in terms of nursing development their profession was suffering from severe stagnation. The civilian nursing hierarchy even as late as the 1970s relied upon "a system of ranks and job specification" rather than on an educational knowledge base supported by research into the value of nursing practice.

Even the WHO commented that, although British nurses were among the best practical nurses in the world, they were very poorly educated. However, part of the problem centred on the fact that the British NHS relied too heavily on the hospital to maintain civilian health. This problem had originated with doctors not nurses. Doctors relied on "curative" rather than "preventative" treatments in order to establish their individual reputations, and used their prestige to persuade government ministers that funds should be concentrated within the hospital environment.

But it can also be argued that the framework for providing civilian health care was in itself a distortion of the military model of healthcare delivery. The Emergency Hospital Scheme established during the war had laid the foundations for the NHS, as had the Civil Nursing Reserve. But the civilian was ignored by the NHS until his or her illness required attention. In much the same way, the soldier was expected to be healthy until he was injured on the battlefield. The military, however, also concentrated on keeping the soldiers fit for combat. Therefore, there was a greater emphasis on health education and preventative medicine within the military environment. The conclusion to be drawn from these different approaches is that the soldier was always expected to be fit for battle, while the civilian was not necessarily expected to be fit for industry.

It was clear, however, that in postwar Britain civilian organisations were based to some extent on military lines simply because the military was perceived to be efficient. This perception centred on the fact that orders were given in the military and usually followed to the letter. The problem with the perception of military efficiency was that no one questioned whether or not the orders themselves were efficient in the first place.

If the NHS was less than ideal, and governed for the most part by senior members of the medical profession, then nurses needed strong leadership in order to make their presence felt. Strong leaders did exist, but they were based in Whitehall and cut off from the rank and file of the profession. Since most nurses tended to follow the leadership of their hospital matrons, rather than the nurses in Whitehall, there was an unbridgeable gap in the formation of civilian nursing policy. Moreover, the profession's overriding concern with nurse status seemed to overshadow all other issues, including those that affected patients.

There was no such gap within the military nursing sector. The chain of command between the Matron-in-Chief and her subordinates was always intact and, because military nurses had successfully resolved their status issues and had taken on board the correct interpretations of the officer role, nursing policy was more geared up to the needs of patients. Ironically, the actual formation of military nursing policy was a more democratic process than could be found in the civilian nursing sector. The Matron-in-Chief paid as much attention to views that emanated from below as she did to views that she imposed from above. It should be noted, however, that military women generally competed at this time on the same terms as some men. That is to say, they were single and without children.

Nevertheless, throughout the nursing profession overall standards of care were difficult to maintain. The military continued to have growing overseas commitments and civilian nurses continued to suffer from the same levels of staff shortages that had been such a prominent feature of the war years. But in terms of professional expectations, the experiences of the military and civilian nurse were worlds apart by 1950. Military nurses had grown used to the fact that they were allowed a good deal of professional autonomy. They were able to prescribe certain drugs, such as morphine, and give intravenous injections, while their civilian colleagues were fighting to be allowed to take a patient's blood pressure.

Despite this divergence in nursing practice, however, most nurses were committed to their patients and to their country. On her return to England after the war, Matron Cocking announced, with regard to military nurses, "Life has been dull since my return but there is not one nurse I know who would not do it all over again in order to have back the England that we once knew." Of course, civilian nurses had also played a significant role in Britain's war effort but, ultimately, in the postwar

246

world the differences between military and civilian nursing boiled down to money: Matron Cocking's dullness of postwar experience reflected the fact that a cash-starved NHS simply could not offer the diversity of professional nursing experience because, as an institution, it needed to reproduce uniform care at the lowest possible cost for the patient.

The military needed to have more highly trained and diverse nurses; without them it was not possible to provide the medical support for the mainstay of Britain's defence. Since military campaigns relied heavily on medical back-up, funds for such diversity were provided by the Ministry of Defence. Although the need for diversity was just as great in the civilian field, particularly in the area of public health and preventative medicine, the Ministry of Health was unable to find adequate funds for such variance. Just as during the war civilian health-care needs were subordinated to those of the emergency services, during peacetime they were still accorded a lower priority but for different reasons. Civilian nurses, who had after all also nursed wartime casualties, thus became themselves one of the inevitable casualties in a system which was committed to modernisation without the commitment of resources commensurate with this responsibility."

APPENDIX 1

1939

31 August: The British government issues orders to evacuate forthwith. As a result, over 3¹/₂ million men, women and children are evacuated from large urban cities to safer rural areas in preparation for war.

1 September: German forces invade Poland, and Britain issues Germany with an ultimatum under the terms of the Anglo-Polish alliance.

3 September: Britain and France declare war on Germany.

17 September: Russian troops enter Eastern Poland. (Russia had signed a non-aggression pact with Germany, which was supposed to guarantee that Germany would not invade Russian territory.)

28 September: Poland is divided by Germany and Russia.

30 November: Russia invades Finland.

17 December: The last of the German "pocket battleships", the *Graf Spee*, is scuttled at Montevideo on the orders of the German High Command. (This move was taken to avoid the embarrassing propaganda that would have ensued if the German population had found out that the ship had been severely damaged by the British Royal Navy during the Battle of the River Plate.)

1940

12 March: Peace Treaty is signed between Russia and Finland.

9 April: German forces invade Denmark and Norway.

10 May: Germans invade Netherlands, Belgium, and Luxembourg. Chamberlain resigns and Churchill takes his place as the British prime minister.

12 May: German forces cross the French border.

15 May: The Dutch Army surrenders.

26 May to 4 June: The Dunkirk evacuation of British troops, during which nearly 900 ships, some in private ownership, ferried 338,226 troops from Dunkirk back to Britain.

28 May: King Leopold surrenders Belgium.

10 June: Italy enters the war on the side of Germany and declares war on Britain and France.

14 June: German forces take over Paris.

15 and 16 June: Russian forces capture Lithuania, Latvia and Estonia.

22 June: France and Germany sign an armistice.

10 July: The start of the Battle of Britain.

7 September: The start of the Blitz.

28 October: Italy invades Greece.

1941

10 January: America introduces a lend-lease policy into Congress which offers financial support for Britain's war effort.

30 March: German forces mount a counter-offensive in North Africa.

6 April: Germany invades Greece and Yugoslavia.

11 April: The Russians sign a Neutrality Treaty with Japan.

20 May: German forces invade Crete.

1 June: The British withdraw from Crete.

8 June: British and Free French forces enter Syria.

14 June: Roosevelt freezes German and Italian funds in America.

22 June: Germany invades Russia, ending the terms of the non-aggression pact.

12 July: Britain and Russia sign a mutual aid pact.

14 August: The Atlantic Charter: Roosevelt and Churchill meet at sea to discuss war aims.

25 August: British and Russian troops enter Iran.

19 September: Germany captures Kiev.

11 October: General Tojo becomes Japan's premier.

18 November: The British Eighth Army begins a desert offensive in Libya.

28 November: Russian forces recapture Rostov.

1 December: The Russians stage a counter-offensive at Tula.

7 December: Japan attacks Pearl Harbor and destroys America's Pacific Fleet. Japan declares war on America and Britain.

8 December: Japanese forces land at Thailand and Malaya. America and Britain declare war on Japan.

9 December: Britain's HMS *Prince of Wales* and HMS *Repulse* are destroyed by Japanese aircraft off the coast of Malaya.

10 and 11 December: Germany and Italy declare war on America, and the latter declares war on the former two.

13 December: Bulgaria and Hungary declare war on America.

22 December: Japan begins a major offensive in the Philippines, and Churchill attends the First Washington Conference.

25 December: Hong Kong surrenders.

1942

1 January: The United Nations Declaration is signed by twenty-six nations. (The Declaration effectively provided an alliance which pledged the military and economic support of the signatories against Germany and Italy. The Declaration also formed the basis of the United Nations Organisation, which was established after hostilities had ceased.)

10 and 11 January: Japanese forces invade the Dutch East Indies.

21 January: German forces stage a counter-offensive in North Africa.

15 February: Singapore falls to the Japanese. The British are forced to surrender the island.

7 March: The evacuation of Rangoon.

17 March: The American General MacArthur arrives in Australia to discuss Allied war aims in the Far East.

9 April: The American forces on Bataan surrender.

18 April: American aircraft launch bombing raids on Tokyo.

4 to 9 May: Battle of the Coral Sea.

26 May: Yet another German counter-offensive in North Africa.

30 to 31 May: The first RAF "thousand bomber raid", under the command of Air Marshal Harris, takes place on Cologne.

4 June: Battle of Midway island.

21 June: Germany captures Tobruk.

25 to 27 June: Second Washington Conference between Roosevelt and Churchill.

7 August: American forces land at Guadalcanal.

12 August: First Moscow Conference.

23 October: Montgomery strikes at El Alamein.

7 and 8 November: American and British undertake a massive reinforcement of their troops in North Africa.

19 to 22 November: The Russians stage a counter-offensive at Stalingrad.

1943

14 to 24 January: Casablanca Conference. Attended by Churchill, Roosevelt and their Chiefs of Staff. Stalin did not attend as he was preoccupied with military campaigns near Stalingrad.

23 January: The British Eighth Army enters Tripoli.

2 February: The German force surrenders at Stalingrad.

2 March: Battle of the Bismark Sea.

11 to 27 May: Third Washington Conference between Roosevelt and Churchill.

12 May: German and Italian resistance in Tunisia finishes.

18 May: United Nations Food Conference takes place in Virginia.

5 July: Battle of Kursk begins. (The Russians eventually pushed back the Germans and were able to move onto the offensive along the whole of the Eastern Front. This battle signified a dramatic turning-point in the war in Europe.)

9 and 10 July: Britain and American forces invade Sicily.

19 July: Bombing raids begin on Rome.

25 July: Mussolini is replaced by Badoglio as Italy's premier.

17 to 24 August: First Quebec Conference. Attended by Churchill, Roosevelt and their Chief's of Staff: Stalin declined to attend.

3 September: British and American forces invade Italy.

8 September: Italy surrenders.

9 September: British and American forces land at Salerno.

10 September: German forces occupy Rome.

13 October: Italy declares war on Germany.

6 November: The Russians recapture Kiev.

9 November: The United Nations Relief and Rehabilitation Administration is formed.

12 December: The Czecho-Russian alliance is formed.

1944

22 January: British and American forces land behind German lines at Anzio.

8 March: The Finns reject the terms of the Russian armistice.

19 March: German forces cross the Hungarian border.

10 April: The Russians retake Odessa.

23 May: British and American troops launch an offensive from Anzio beachhead.

4 June: Rome is captured by British and American troops.

6 June: D-Day: British and American invasion of Normandy.

13 and 14 June: The first Vl flying bombs (doodlebugs) land in Britain.

15 June: The first American B-29 Superfortress raid takes place on Japan.

3 July: The Russians recapture Minsk.

27 July: American troops break through west of St-Lo.

11 August: American forces occupy Guam.

15 August: British and American troops land on the French south coast.

25 August: Paris is liberated.

3 September: Brussels is liberated.

8 September: The first V2 rocket lands on London.

17 September: American and British troops land in Holland.

14 October: American and British troops occupy Athens.

20 October: Belgrade is liberated, and American troops invade the Philippines.

21 and 22 October: Battle of Leyte Gulf.

12 November: *Tirpitz* is sunk by the RAF.

16 December: The Germans launch their last major counter-offensive — Battle of the Bulge.

1945

9 January: American forces land on Luzon in the Philippines.

11 January: The Russians take Warsaw.

20 January: Hungary signs armistice.

27 January: Memel is liberated.

31 January: Churchill and Roosevelt meet at Malta.

3 February: American troops enter Manila.

4 to 12 February: Conference held at Yalta between Roosevelt, Stalin and Churchill.

19 February: American troops land on Iwo Jima.

7 March: The American First Army crosses the Rhine.

1 April: America invades Okinawa.

12 April: Roosevelt dies and is replaced as American president by Truman.

13 April: Vienna is liberated.

28 April: Mussolini is executed by partisan forces.

30 April: Hitler commits suicide in his bunker in Berlin; American forces liberate 33,000 inmates at Dachau concentration camp; and the Russian flag is raised over the Reichstag in Berlin.

1 May: Admiral Doenitz assumes command of Germany.

2 May: Berlin falls to the Russians.

3 May: Rangoon is captured.

7 May: Germany surrenders.

8 May: Victory in Europe Day.

17 July to 2 August: Potsdam Conference. Attended by Churchill, Truman and Stalin.

6 August: The atomic bomb is dropped on Hiroshima.

8 August: Russia declares war on Japan.

9 August: The second atomic bomb is dropped, on Nagasaki.

14 August: Japan surrenders.

2 September: Japanese sign surrender terms in Tokyo Bay.

APPENDIX 2

K EY E VENTS FOR N URSES

1939
The government abolishes the minimum educational qualification for entry to nurse training to encourage recruitment.

Athlone Interim Report advises the government that to improve nurse recruitment nurses need to work shorter hours and receive better and nationally formulated pay scales. The government also needs to subsidise hospitals in order to standardise nurse training.

With the outbreak of war, there is a massive unrestricted flow of nurses into the forces, which leaves the civilian nursing services sadly depleted in number and experience.

Dame Katherine Jones launches her militarisation policy.

1940
The disorganised and badly trained Civil Nursing Reserve is giving cause for concern, and nursing services are on the point of breakdown.

Complaints from VADs working in the armed forces prompt concessions from the Army Council.

1941

The government creates Senior Nursing Officer positions at Whitehall in an attempt to resolve the civilian nursing crisis. Conscription is extended to include women.

State registered nurses working in the armed forces are awarded Commissioned Officer status.

1942

There is still a desperate shortage of nurses, despite the fact that the role of the Civil Nursing Reserve has been extended to include all nursing areas rather than just the emergency services.

1943

Rushcliffe Committee introduces national pay scales and increases the divergence in pay between trained and untrained staff.

Controversial Nurses Act gives official recognition to the "assistant nurse" but also contains a clause allowing Christian Science nurses to call themselves nurses without any formal training.

The government restricts the flow of certain categories of trained nurses into the forces in an attempt to alleviate the shortages in civilian nursing services.

For the first time, nurses are brought under the Control of Engagement Act. This move allows the Ministry of

Labour to direct nurses to work in areas of great nursing shortages. A clause in the Act, however, states that if nurses enter further training on qualifying for registered status they could avoid such direction.

The Army launches a takeover bid of the voluntary services in an effort to resolve the VAD status and task allocation crisis.

1944

As Britain begins to wage war on a "Second Front", the armed forces are in desperate need of more nurses. Because of the recruiting restrictions introduced in 1943, the forces are only able to recruit newly qualified and inexperienced nurses.

1945

As hostilities cease in Europe in May and in the Far East in August, it is estimated that over 3,000 nurses have died as a result of the conflicts.

Nurses captured and incarcerated by the Japanese are released.

Nurses begin working with the United Nations Relief and Rehabilitation Association to resettle refugees and other victims of war.

At home, the continuing shortage of nurses threatens to scupper the plans for a National Health Service.

APPENDIX 3

NOTES ON SOURCES

The bulk of the material used to write this book has been obtained from nurses themselves: from military and civilian nurses, who kindly recounted their stories for the BBC Radio 4 programme *Frontline Females*, and from the letters and diaries of wartime nurses, which are housed in the Public Record Office (PRO) and the Imperial War Museum. Oral history transcripts have also been personally obtained by the author. Additional material has been found in the hospital archives of some of the more major city hospitals, most notably the Royal London Hospital, the Great Ormond Street Hospital for Sick Children, the Radcliffe Infirmary, Oxford, the Bristol Royal Infirmary and hospitals in Newcastle and Glasgow. These archives contain not only the matrons' minutes of the period, but also the views of many ordinary nurses. These views were expressed in the hospital magazines of the time.

The Ministry of Health, Ministry of Labour, the General Nursing Council (GNC) and the War Office (WO) records have all been consulted at the PRO, and these records have been supplemented by material obtained from the Royal College of Nursing (RCN) archives, Edinburgh. More detailed research on military nursing has concentrated on those records housed at the Queen Alexandra's Royal Army Nursing Corps

Museum, Aldershot, and the Red Cross Museum, Guildford. Understandably, some records have been lost as a result of military activity, and all nurses' letters were governed by strict censorship rules. These rules were enforced so that strategic positions could not be revealed should letters accidentally fall into enemy hands. However, despite these limitations, letters did yield valuable information regarding the wartime attitudes of nurses and their postwar expectations.

Hansard debates with regard to the nursing crisis were examined in depth. Moreover, contemporary journals and newspapers were also consulted at length. Of these, the *British Journal of Nursing* proved to be the most useful. It was not by any means the only nursing journal of the period, but it was the only one that remained constantly attuned, both to the global wartime political situation and to the more mundane problems faced by nurses themselves. While the *Nursing Illustrated* and other nursing periodicals relayed to their readers the virtues of beauty treatments, or introduced them to new wartime recipes, the *British Journal of Nursing* kept its readership up to date with current affairs and medical developments. As such the paper appeared to represent the views of nurses who were politically aware and professionally motivated. Finally, in order to get a clearer picture of how military nursing developed in the postwar years, several interviews were conducted with senior nursing officers currently working within the present-day armed forces.

INDEX

ISIS publish a wide range of books in large print, from fiction to biography. A full list of titles is available free of charge from the address below. Alternatively, contact your local library for details of their collection of ISIS large print books.

Details of ISIS complete and unabridged audio books are also available.

Any suggestions for books you would like to see in large print or audio are always welcome.

7 Centremead
Osney Mead
Oxford OX2 0ES
(01865) 250333